INSTAGRAM HACKS

© **Copyright 2019 by Jacob Nicholson - All rights reserved.**

This document is geared towards providing exact and reliable information in regards to the topic and issue covered. The publication is sold with the idea that the publisher is not required to render accounting, officially permitted, or otherwise, qualified services. If advice is necessary, legal or professional, a practiced individual in the profession should be ordered.

- From a Declaration of Principles which was accepted and approved equally by a Committee of the American Bar Association and a Committee of Publishers and Associations.

In no way is it legal to reproduce, duplicate, or transmit any part of this document in either electronic means or printed format. The recording of this publication is strictly prohibited, and any storage of this document is not allowed unless with written permission from the publisher. All rights reserved.

The information provided herein is stated to be truthful and consistent, in that any liability, in terms of inattention or otherwise, by any usage or abuse of any policies, processes, or directions contained within is the solitary and utter responsibility of the recipient reader. Under no circumstances will any legal responsibility or blame be held against the publisher for any reparation, damages, or monetary loss due to the information herein, either directly or indirectly.

Respective authors own all copyrights not held by the publisher.

The information herein is offered for informational purposes solely and is universal as so. The presentation of the information is without a contract or any guarantee assurance.

The trademarks that are used are without any consent, and the publication of the trademark is without permission or backing by the trademark owner. All trademarks and brands within this book are for clarifying purposes only and are owned by the owners themselves, not affiliated with this document.

Table of Contents

INTRODUCTION 1

INSTAGRAM 5

HISTORY OF INSTAGRAM 11

HOW INSTAGRAM WORKS... 14

ADVANTAGES AND DISADVANTAGES OF INSTAGRAM...... 25

INSTAGRAM FEATURES.. 32

INSTAGRAM TERMINOLOGY 43

INSTAGRAM HANDLE... 51

INSTAGRAM HANDLE FOR BUSINESSES............................ 53

THINGS YOU NEED TO DO WHEN GETTING STARTED ON INSTAGRAM 57

THE INSTAGRAM DO'S AND DON'TS 65

INSTAGRAM FOR BUSINESS 68

REASONS TO USE INSTAGRAM FOR YOUR BUSINESS........ 92

TIPS FOR MASTERING INSTAGRAM FOR BUSINESS.......... 103

HOW TO CREATE AN INSTAGRAM BUSINESS PROFILE 111

DOS AND DON'TS OF INSTAGRAM MARKETING 119

STEPS TO EFFECTIVELY USE INSTAGRAM TO GENERATE SALES 128

INSTAGRAM HACKS 134

INSTAGRAM FOR BUSINESS HACKS................................ 187

INTRODUCTION

Instagram is an online mobile application that is used for sharing photos and videos. Instagram is following in the footsteps of Facebook and Twitter, and has fast become a very popular social media tool. Instagram was originally developed so that people could apply different filters to photographs they had taken on their mobile phones and would allow them to easily upload and share these photos with friends (or account followers) using the Instagram application. More recently video was introduced to Instagram; it can now be uploaded, but Instagram video clips are limited to or between 3 to 15 seconds long.

There are more than 300 million Instagram users worldwide. Approximately, 70 million photos are uploaded per day. The account is 'free' to set up so there are low barriers to entry. It is a medium that allows for easy sharing of content 24 hours a day.

Businesses such as Levis, L'oreal, and hundreds of others have been able to use the tool to:

To increase awareness of their products and services.

To increase brand recognition.

To showcase their community and pro bono work to inspire and attract prospective customers to engage with their product, service or brand.

Run successful promotions, competitions, and giveaways.

Instagram appears to be particularly popular with product based businesses due to its visual nature. Many businesses that are product-based, such as clothing, jewellery, make up, or even food-based businesses have achieved success using Instagram. This is because the application allows photos to be posted and shared to people either wearing or using these products. For instance, a food manufacturer might post photos of someone cooking with, sharing a meal, or entertaining friends using their food products. This success is not exclusive to big brands as many small businesses have been able to leverage the power of Instagram to engage their clients.

Bloggers, social media stars, and media personalities have amassed a loyal following online with hundreds and sometimes thousands of people following their Instagram accounts. This 'influencer' group means that there are several eyeballs there ready to see your product or service. The audience has been built for you already. The engagement has already been formed and tapping into this by getting your product uploaded onto their Instagram feed or featured by a blogger or popular Instagram account holder will help you to grow your audience more quickly. Therefore, taking the time to identify key 'influencers' in your industry and how you can tap into this is important.

Hashtags are tags that you can add in a caption of a photo that you upload. To create a hashtag you need to use the # symbol at the front of the tag and then add a keyword or several keywords without spaces after the hash symbol. For example, you might post a product image of pair of jeans. Your hashtags could be: #fashion #style #jeans #lovethatstyle. You may already be familiar with hashtags as they are also popular on Twitter, but if you are not taking a look online to see some examples of how they are being used. The purpose of the hashtag is to tag your photo to a subject or topic category that is 'searchable' or 'popular' on Instagram.

Some hashtags are very popular, so it's important to identify the ones that are most relevant to your industry. The aim of the game is to get people talking, liking, following, and sharing your content. Hashtags help to get the word out if used effectively. So, take some time to find out how to use these to get the best out of your content.

Instagram includes a powerful search feature, so if posts are set to 'public,' you can use hashtags to tag your photos and videos so that the content becomes easier to search and becomes more accessible to the public. That means when someone runs a search and is exploring that 'search term,' your content may be discovered, which leads to more people finding out about your business or brand.

INSTAGRAM

Instagram is a photo sharing app which allows users to assign filters to photos and share them with followers. Instagram rolled out a desktop site this year for browsing (not uploading), but the app continues to be a preferred environment for users to interact.

Users follow each other in an asynchronous manner, like Twitter, and can comment, like, and tag each other in pictures. Instagram also has map check in and hashtag capability to allow users to search by topic.

Instagramers can sync their photo sharing to other social networks so that Instagram photos can be posted directly to Facebook, Tumblr, Twitter, Flickr, and Foursquare.

Similar to Facebook or Twitter, everyone who creates an Instagram account has a profile and a news feed.

When you post a photo or video on Instagram, it will be displayed on your profile. Other users who follow you will see your posts in their feed.

Likewise, you'll see posts from other users whom you choose to follow.

It's like a simplified version of Facebook, with an emphasis on mobile use and visual sharing. Just like other social networks, you can interact with other users on Instagram by following them, being followed by them, commenting, liking, tagging, and private messaging. You can even save the photos you see on Instagram.

Instagram is available for free on iOS devices, like the iPhone and iPad, as well as Android devices, like phones and tablets from Google, Samsung, etc.

It can also be accessed on the web from a computer, but users can only upload and share photos or videos from their devices.

Before you can start using the app, Instagram will ask you to create a free account. You can sign up via your existing Facebook account or by email. All you need is a username and a password.

You may be asked if you want to follow some friends who are on Instagram in your Facebook network. You can do this right away or skip through the process and come back to it later.

It's always a good idea to customize your profile by adding your name, a photo, a short bio, and a website link if you have one when you first get on Instagram. When you start following people and looking for people to follow you back, they'll want to know who you are, and what you're all about.

As previously mentioned, Instagram is all about visual sharing, so everybody intend to share and find only the best photos and videos. Every user profile has a "Followers" and "Following" count, which represents how many people they follow and how many other users are following them.

Every user profile has a button you can tap to follow them. If a user has their profile set to private, they will need to approve your request first.

Keep in mind that when your profile is created and set to public, anyone can find and view your profile, along with all your photos and videos. Set yours to private if you only want the followers you approve to be able to see your posts.

Interacting on posts is fun and easy. You can double-tap any post to "like" it, or add a comment at the bottom. You can even click the arrow button to share it with someone via direct message.

If you want to find or add more friends or interesting accounts to follow, use the search tab (marked by the magnifying glass icon) to browse through tailored posts recommended to you. You can also use the search bar at the top to look for specific users or hashtags.

Instagram has come a long way since its early days in terms of posting options. When it's first launched in 2010, users could only post photos through the app and add filters without any extra editing features.

Today, you can post either directly through the app or from existing photos/videos on your device. You can also post both photos and videos up to one full minute in length, and you have a whole bunch of extra filter options plus the ability to tweak and edit.

When you tap the middle of the Instagram posting tab, you can select the camera or video icon to let the app know whether you want to post a photo or a video. Capture it through the app, or tap the photo/video preview box to pull up a previously captured one.

Instagram has up to 23 filters you can choose to apply to both photos and videos. By tapping the Edit option at the bottom of the photo editor, you can also apply editing effects allowing you to edit adjustments, brightness, contrast, and structure. For videos, you can trim them and select a cover frame.

If you want to edit your photo or video within the Instagram app, simply tap the wrench icon and choose a feature from the bottom menu. You can adjust the contrast, warmth, saturation, highlights, shadows, vignette, tilt-shift, and sharpness.

After you've applied an optional filter and possibly made some edits, you'll be taken to a tab where you can fill out a caption, tag other users to it, tag it to a geographical location and simultaneously post it to some of your other social networks.

Once it's published, your followers will be able to view it and interact with it in their feeds. You can always delete your posts or edit their details after you published them by tapping the three dots at the top.

You can configure your Instagram account to have photos posted on Facebook, Twitter, Tumblr or Flickr. If these sharing configurations are all highlighted, as opposed to remaining gray and inactive, then all of your Instagram photos will automatically be posted to your social networks after you press Share. If you don't want your photo shared on any particular social network, simply tap any one of them so that it's gray and set to off.

Instagram has a Stories feature, which is a secondary feed that appears at the very top of your main feed. You can see it marked by little photo bubbles of the users you follow.

To publish your story, all you have to do is tap your photo bubble from the main feed, or swipe right on any tab to access the stories camera tab.

HISTORY OF INSTAGRAM

Instagram was started in San Francisco by Kevin Systrom and Mike Krieger, who initially tried creating a platform similar to Foursquare, but then turned their attention exclusively to photo sharing. The word Instagram is an amalgam of "instant camera," and "telegram."

The iOS app was released through the iTunes App Store on Oct. 6, 2010, and the Android app was released on April 3, 2012. The platform's popularity skyrocketed, with the company reporting more than 40 million active users within two years after launch. This caught the attention of Facebook, which officially purchased Instagram for $1 billion in the summer of 2012.

Originally, only photos could be posted to Instagram, but the company expanded to 15-second videos in 2013. In 2016, Instagram upped the maximum video length to 60 seconds. Until 2015, all photos posted to Instagram were confined to a square aspect ratio. The company changed this to allow users to upload photos and video at full size.

Following heavy backlash from users who feared Instagram would sell their photos and identifiers, CEO Systrom assured users that wasn't the company's intention. The language was quickly removed from the policy.

A 2013 controversy centered around criticisms that Instagram was censoring photos that didn't break the company's terms and conditions, and that these censorships were unfairly targeting women's bodies. Instagram's decision in 2016 to shift from displaying timeline photos in chronological order to using an algorithm to determine photo order also drew negative feedback.

As of April 2017, the company had 700 million active users, more than twice that of Twitter's total user base.

Instagram provides a wide range of digital filters that can be applied to users' photos, including ones that add a vintage or faded look. Other editing features include Lux, an effect that lightens shadows, darkens highlight, and increases contrast, and photo-tuning tools allow users to adjust brightness, contrast, saturation, sharpness, structure, straightness, and tint. A manual tilt shift and vignette effect can also be added to photos.

In 2017, Instagram rolled out a feature that allows users to post multiple photos or videos at once, presented in a carousel format.

Taking inspiration from the popular Snapchat app, Instagram introduced a Stories feature in 2016 that allows users to share moments from their day that disappear after 24 hours. Instagram Stories includes the ability to incorporate augmented reality-based face filters and stickers and the ability to add text, drawings, emojis, links and geotags directly to the photo or video. In April 2017, Instagram Stories recorded 200 million active users, surpassing the active users of Snapchat, its biggest rival.

Instagram also has a series of add-on apps available. These apps are Boomerang, which creates custom GIFs; Hyperlapse, which creates time-lapse videos; and Layout, which creates image collages with multiple images. When installed, these apps can be accessed directly from the Instagram app.

HOW INSTAGRAM WORKS

Instagram has surely come a long way, business-wise, since co-founders Kevin Systrom and Mike Krieger introduced the app in 2010. But on the whole, the app has remained simple, straightforward, and social since its inception.

1. Register / Setup

Instagram has always been an almost exclusively mobile platform. Therefore, you must download the iPhone or Android app to your device to register an Instagram account.

Instagram accounts are public by default, but you may create a private account. In that case, only users who you approve may follow you and view your photos. Head to your profile tab and scroll down to "Privacy." There, you may select to make photos private.

Once registered, change your profile picture and edit your profile information, which includes a brief 150-character bio and a website. You may also edit profile information here.

2. Notifications

Since Instagram doesn't have a web-hosted feed of photos, you'll be doing most of your browsing on mobile. For that reason, you may choose to enrich your mobile experience by setting up push notifications.

Depending on your level of comfort, enable the following push notifications:

When a user likes or comments on one of your photos.

When a user @mentions you in a comment.

When your photo is posted to the Popular page.

When you are tagged in a photo

To control the notifications on your device, click on the Settings wheel while viewing your profile. Scroll down and select Push Notification Settings. You can also edit your Share Settings from the options panel. To change the way you receive notifications from Instagram, exit the app and access the Settings location. From there, find Instagram in the Notification Center and configure your app preferences.

If you choose not to enable external notifications, Instagram would still keep you apprised of your account activity in-app. New user and comment notifications appear in the News section of the app (see above-left), which you can access via the navigation panel — the icon looks like a speech bubble with a heart in it.

3. Connect to Social

Again, because Instagram is a relatively isolated social app that lives inherently on mobile, it's important to connect social accounts to get the most out of the experience. You may choose to link Instagram to your Twitter, Facebook, Foursquare, Tumblr, Flickr, VK, Mixi and Weibo accounts (the latter two apply only to iPhone users in Japan and China respectively).

To connect social accounts, head to the Profile Tab > Edit Sharing Settings, then choose the network you wish to connect.

Each time you upload a photo to Instagram, you'll have the option to share to each of the social networks you've enabled, or to none. If you choose to share to no social networks, the photo would post only to Instagram, viewable only by those users who follow you on the app.

4. Add a Photo

The bread and butter of Instagram are, obviously, sharing photos. Before you explore much else, I suggest you test it out.

Click the blue camera button in the center of your Instagram navigation panel. By default, Instagram activates your device's camera, so you may either choose to snap a picture then and there, or choose a picture already saved to your phone. If you choose the latter, click the double-square button on the lower-left of the screen.

If you choose a photo from your camera roll, keep in mind that Instagram sizes photos to perfect squares. Therefore, if you select a photo that was originally taken horizontally (landscape), you'll have to crop some portions of the image — either that, or live with the default black border.

5. Filters / Borders

Once you've either taken or selected a photo, a set of three icons appears beneath the image. They are the famous Instagram filters which add different pre-determined layers to your pictures, and give the effect that you've altered or professionally edited them. Many filters add "vintage" effects, which have certainly pleased many a hipster.

Scroll through the filters and experiment with the best one for that particular image. You'll soon find that certain filters work well with specific types of photos, whether outdoor panoramas, personal portraits, odd perspectives, intense colors, etc.

Each filter also has its associated border. For instance, the Earlybird filter adds rounded edges to your photo, and Kelvin adds a rough, sandpapery frame. You may, however, choose to forego borders altogether by tapping the square "frame" on the upper-left of the edit screen.

6. Tilt-Shift

Another celebrated editing option on Instagram; tilt-shift allows you to selectively focus certain planes of the photo, almost as if you were using a special DSLR lens. Tilt-shift gives the appearance of an altered depth of field, which can make smartphone snaps look stunning when used wisely.

Experiment with the tilt-shift feature by tapping the button above the photo that looks like a water droplet. From there, choose either the horizontal bar or the circle. The bar adds a thin field of focus across your image, which you may tap and move up and down, or two-finger tap and swivel to rotate. Or move the circle tilt-shift across your photo for a more focused effect.

You'll find that tilt-shift elevates many photos to a professional (and sometimes, artistic) standard. But other times, tilt-shift can seem out of place. Use your best judgment and artistic know-how to determine the effect you're looking for.

7. Other Options

Before saving your photo, test a few other edit options. Tap, the sun icon on the lower-left of the edit screen, to apply the Lux effect — essentially, an auto-enhance button that enriches the colors in your image.

Additionally, the curved arrow to the right of the frame option rotates your image, and the next camera icon flips your camera front-facing so that you can take a picture of yourself.

8. Video

With Instagram video, you can record short video clips ranging anywhere from three to fifteen seconds long. To record video, press the camera button and choose the video recorder option on the right.

Choose to film either one continuous segment or several clips spliced together, which allows for some creative stop-motion or animated videos. To create multiple clips, lift your finger off the record button. If you aren't happy with a previous clip, delete it by pressing the delete arrow.

When you're finished recording your video, click Next to add a filter, exactly as you would a photo, only Instagram Video offers different filter options than photo. For users with the iPhone 4S, or any later iPhone model, this stage also includes a video stabilizing feature. Though turned on by default, stabilization can be toggled off with a single click.

If you don't like the pressure of creating video live, you may choose an existing video in your phone's gallery. iPhone users can upload multiple saved videos, splicing them together.

9. Share

Once your photo is ready to go, click the green checkmark. This brings you to the social sharing screen.

If you wish, add a caption, explaining what you've photographed, an anecdote, or really anything your social networks would enjoy. Feel free to add category hashtags and @mention people, especially if you plan to share via Twitter. The caption will be the text of the tweet, and the app will file hashtags and @mentions accordingly.

If you've enabled location services, you even have the option to tag where you took the photo.

Then, depending on what networks you've linked to Instagram, toggle the accounts to share across those platforms.

The way your photo appears when posted depends on the style of the social network to which you post. When sharing to Facebook, your Instagram photo will appear in the News Feed with the attached caption.

You may also choose to retroactively share the Instagram photos you've already posted. Head to your profile, then select a photo. To share, click the icon on the lower-right of the screen — it has three dots — Choose the "Share post" option and select one of your networks. Or choose "copy URL" to share manually.

10. Follow Users

Now, you're ready to find users to follow. Chances are many of your social media friends are already using Instagram, and on top of that, a bunch of celebrities are, too.

Head to your profile tab and select "Find Friends." You may search for friends who have connected their Facebook and Twitter accounts to Instagram, or you may input your phone's contact list to generate further connections. Or search by name, username or tag (e.g. "#skydiving").

Finally, Instagram does a great job curating suggested users and trending photos. Head to the Popular page (see right), denoted by the star on your navigation panel, and peruse photos that strike your fancy.

Once you've followed some users, you'll begin to see their photos appear in your news feed, accessed by tapping the icon that looks like a house on the left side of the navigation panel. Alongside user photos, you'll see people who have liked or commented on the photo. Add your own two cents!

11. Using Instagram on the Web

Instagram's presence on the web has improved enormously in the last year. You can now use the web version to do just about everything — edit your profile, comment and like photos, discover and follow other users — except upload pictures and videos.

To access your profile, navigate to Instagram.com and enter your login info.

ADVANTAGES AND DISADVANTAGES OF INSTAGRAM

Advantage

- Massive

Instagram is a social network that has grown widely in recent years. Between Facebook, Twitter, and Instagram, the latter is the one with the highest number of active users per month.

- A picture is worth a thousand words."

The main feature of Instagram is that it allows you to share photos. Sometimes, the images are able to convey more information than a written text.

Images can evoke emotions and feelings. They are also more attractive than other forms of interaction. This establishes a much more effective communication system among users.

- Ideal for virtual stores

Instagram has now become a marketing tool. Many virtual stores employ this platform to promote their products.

Thanks to this platform. The relationship between sellers and buyers is more interactive.

- Privacy and security

One of the most important advantages of Instagram is its privacy and security policy.

Their use is limited to persons over 13 years old, in order to protect children from certain contents that may not be suitable for them.

In addition, it can be established that the publications are private. When choosing this option, the other users who want to see the photos, videos or any other element of the profile should send a follow-up request to the user with the private account. This user has the authority to accept or reject such request.

Finally, if a user is violating the conditions of Instagram, or if it violates the security of other members of the network, then it can be blocked and will not be able to see the publications of those who have blocked it.

- Free

Like other social networks, the Instagram service is free. Neither the subscription nor the download of the application generate additional costs to the derivatives for the payment of Internet service.

- Sharing Options

Instagram lets you share photos and videos that can be created directly from the application, or can be uploaded from the memory of the mobile device.

The application also offers the option of sharing these files on other social networks, such as Twitter and Facebook.

- Communication medium

Being a social network, Instagram is a means of communication. In addition to publishing multimedia files, this application offers instant messaging services.

- Promotes artistic skills

The Instagram social network encourages people's artistic skills. Thanks to this application. Many users are more aware of the fundamental elements of photography: angles, planes, focus, among others.

Disadvantages

- Designed to be portable

The Instagram application was created as a portable system. That is, its design is best suited for mobile devices, such as smartphones and tablets.

There is a web version of this social network that can be used on desktop computers, but does not offer as many services as the mobile application.

- Not compatible with all operating systems

The Instagram application is only available for iOS, Android, and Windows Mobile operating systems.

This excludes people who have devices with BlackBerry systems, OS, and Linux, among others.

- Limited tools for editing images

To be a network that is based on the publication of images, it has limited tools for editing these files.

It only has a couple of dozen effects (filters), and additional options must be downloaded separately.

- Possibility of image theft

By posting quality or professional images on a social network, it is possible for someone to access them and use them for professional issues of which they benefit economically.

Therefore, there is a possibility of "stealing" images to a user without their consent.

- The privacy of the images is collective, not individual

You cannot configure the privacy of each photo individually. This means that there are only two options: that all publications are public or all are private.

- Addictive

The Instagram social network can become an addiction for its users. For this reason, it must be used with caution.

- False advertising

Many stores rely on Instagram to promote their products and services. Sometimes, these accounts resort to false advertising to attract customers. This can generate mistrust on the part of the users.

- Depends on the images

The popularity of an account is largely based on the quality of the published images. If the photos are not attractive enough, then the account will not have as many followers.

In the case of virtual stores, if the photos of the products fail to convey the benefits of these, then the store will not generate sales.

INSTAGRAM FEATURES

Instagram has become one of the most popular social media platforms, and has a massive user base. The social network had over one billion active monthly users. This means the platform's user base has gotten too big for any brand or marketer to ignore. It has become an important social media marketing platform crawling with influencers, brands, and marketers.

Luckily, Instagram is geared towards businesses and all its features can readily be used for marketing purposes, whether you're looking to buy ads or market organically. With a more youthful audience and the largest percentage of users falling in the age range of 18-34 (64%), these features are built to catch the eye of the young people who primarily use it. No wonder Instagram already has over 25 million business accounts. 44% of Instagram's active users use the platform for researching and discovering brands, making it the place to be if you have a business or are marketing a brand. And the great thing is you don't have to spend one cent to market your business on Instagram. With all its great features that lean itself towards marketing, it's as simple as pie to do.

- **Filters**

Instagram's photo filters are central to its success. Their ability to turn anyone into a professional photographer is what drew people to the platform in the first place. Each one of the 40 filters creates a different look and feel, so you can decide which one best represents your brand. If you are marketing a business, you want your content to be consistent in terms of brand image and style. This way, your followers will be able to identify your content and get to know your signature look.

One way to do this is to manage your preferred filters by selecting the gear icon at the end of the filter list. If more than one person manages the account, this will make it easy to identify which filters you use regularly and make sure everyone is on the same page.

- **Video posts**

Long gone are the days that video marketing was only for companies with big budgets. Anyone with a decent camera and basic know-how is now a video marketer , and an estimated 81% of businesses used video as a marketing tool. In addition, "Engagement numbers for videos posted to top media publisher accounts worldwide increased by 53% year over year in May, surpassing the 46% growth rate seen for photos over the same timeframe."

While video is great for increasing engagement; it also gives you the ability to share more complex, in-depth content that can't be conveyed in one image or series of Stories. Initially limited to 15 seconds, video posts today allow businesses to create long-form, high-production value videos of up to 1 minute long that leads to lots of engagement. You can also schedule Instagram videos just like regular Instagram posts, mostly using third party apps.

Instagram videos that convey your brand message or introduce your company culture are a great way to build trust with your followers and customers. Make sure to make the first few seconds of your video captivating so that you can catch people's interest before they click away.

PRO TIP: Remember that you are trying to grab users' attention in the first few seconds of your video, so make sure they are understandable even without sound! Many users watch videos in places where they are unable to listen to the sound, and your marketing content should always keep that in mind.

Instagram Stories

The addition of Stories has been huge for Instagram. The feature, which was added in 2016, was initially thought to be a copy of Snapchat's hugely successful model. But it has since skyrocketed in popularity and with businesses increasingly looking for tools to increase engagement with their brands without having to make massive investments in creative content, Stories, with all its features included, are gold.

Stories appear as little circles in the top of your followers' feeds and disappear after 24 hours, which makes it a fun and less stylized. For marketing purposes, Stories are particularly useful to showcase new products or releases, promotions, employees, workplace culture or team outings. A great way to encourage more people to follow you on Instagram is to offer Stories-only giveaways and promotions. Here is a list of ways to use Instagram Stories like an expert.

✓ **Stories Highlights**

Instagram Stories are a great feature, but they disappear after 24 hours. While, the transience of Stories is what, made them so successful, users expressed a desire to keep some of their best stories for later use. So Instagram created the Stories Highlights feature. This allows you to save your best stories, and keep them on your account as long as you want. Instagram saves your Stories Highlights at the top of your profile page so that your followers and anyone else who visits your Instagram profile is able to see them.

There are various ways to use this feature for marketing purposes. You can create stories with promotions, information about your business, or that showcase specific products or events. Stories with quizzes are also great to educate followers about your brand and gather information about their preferences. Remember to save your best performing stories as well so that you can continue to drive people to see them, and preferably take the action you want them to take.

Instagram Stories video

Video in Instagram Stories can be highly entertaining, and is great for building engagement, creating brand awareness, and driving traffic to your website. Videos on Instagram Stories only last 15 seconds, so your clips need to be short and catchy. Instagram introduced a workaround for the short Stories video by allowing video to run over into the next clip after 15 seconds. This opened the feature up for even more potential uses. Use it for fun and promotional content that reflects your brand's tone and style.

PRO TIP: If you want to get the most from your Stories videos, think about creating branded stories that have all have the same color, tone, style, and format. There are now design Instagram Stories templates to make your life easy in this regard.

Instagram Live

Instagram Live has been part of the Stories feature since its roll-out. Initially received with some uncertainty about how to use this feature, businesses and marketers have taken to it with great creativity to create hype around their products. Because of its transient nature, there is a sense of urgency among users to watch your live broadcast before it disappears. You can use this to your advantage. Offer promotions, discounts, or giveaways during your live broadcast, but promote it with short clips or posts beforehand so that your followers are compelled to watch your broadcast.

Instagram Live is also great for generating leads. You can ask your followers to submit their questions about whatever topic you'll be discussing during the live broadcast beforehand. Use the "Ask me anything" sticker in Instagram Stories to easily gather questions. You can then answer them live. Your followers will love you for mentioning them, and the real-time interaction is great for your brand exposure.

- ✓ **AR filters**

Despite how futuristic the name might sound, AR (short for "augmented reality") is already being used in many places. AR is a technology that superimposes virtual effects (generated by a computer) onto real images and video when using a camera. On Instagram, these AR filters are known as face filters. They are whimsical, and cute overlays you can add to your photos and videos via Instagram Stories.

Facebook (the owner of Instagram) recently started partnering with strategic brands to create unique, interactive camera experiences, including face filters and world effects, for their followers on Instagram. Where Instagram previously controlled all the AR filters, select brands can now create their custom AR filters for Instagram Stories and these may soon be rolled out to all users.

One of the first businesses to create custom AR filters for Instagram was the Kardashians' youngest billionaire, Kylie Jenner's Kylie Cosmetics. When you choose the Kylie Cosmetics AR filter in Instagram Stories, you can "try on" different lipsticks from Kylie's Lip Kits to see which shade you like before buying it. This is an example of how a business can use custom AR filters to market their brand. It's fun, not overly promotional and helpful if you're looking to buy the product. Besides, users will only be able to access your filter if they follow your brand on Instagram, or visit your profile to try it out. As Instagram allows more third parties to create their custom AR filters, brands have an amazing new tool at their disposal for advertising and promoting themselves on Instagram.

✓ **IGTV**

The latest and arguably one of the most exciting additions to Instagram's features is Instagram TV. Launched as Instagram's first standalone video platform, IGTV is an entire new channel for businesses to grow their following, and increase their engagement. Before you can upload an IGTV video to your feed, you need to create an IGTV channel. This is easy enough and you create an account with your Instagram account. IGTV video will now be in the grid of your Instagram profile, with the IGTV icon in the right-hand corner. While the sky truly is the limit for what you can do with IGTV, in terms of marketing it's great for promoting products, creating how product tutorials and for sharing news – think of the video you would see on YouTube.

Your videos don't have to be professionally shot, and can be about anything! It's like an improvement from your Instagram Stories, but it doesn't have to be as perfect or curated like an Instagram post or video would be. Instagram offers analytics for your IGTV video and measures views, likes, and comments, as well as your audience retention rate, which is how many people, watched your video all the way to the end. These metrics are crucial when strategizing how to make use of IGTV, so it's most effective in terms of marketing. For instance, if your see viewers drop off after 10 minutes, you can take that as a sign that creating videos that are longer than ten minutes is a waste of time and resources.

✓ Stickers and quizzes

Instagram Stories are becoming more polished and elaborate by the day as it introduces new functions. One of the most popular used Stories tools is stickers. From emoji sliders, to polls, and GIFs, these added extras can help you interact with your followers in innovative new ways, and increase engagement.

For example, hashtag stickers have the potential to reach thousands of Instagram users in your region and/or your industry with similar interests. They can also help reiterate a brand message, threading together a campaign. Location stickers can let Instagrammers know where your business is, and question stickers are great for galvanizing your followers, and getting some insight into the things they're most interested in. The latest addition to stickers is quiz stickers, which Instagram added in April 2019.

When a user interacts with one of your stories, it sends a signal to Instagram's algorithm. This signal is then used to rank your stories higher in the user's story carousel. The more engagement you get, the higher your stories will rank. Getting your followers not to view your content but also interact with it is, therefore, key to reaching a greater percentage of your followers. Quiz stickers can also be used to help your audience get to know you and your business. Asking questions specifically related to your business can educate your followers, and help you discover who your biggest fans are.

While all these features individually has great potential for marketing, using a combination of all of them and making them work together will yield the best results for your business or brand.

INSTAGRAM TERMINOLOGY

❖ **Username**

Your username is how people recognize you on Instagram. The name you choose follows the @ symbol, and can include numbers, letters, periods, and underscores. Your username appears atop all the pictures or videos you post and at the top of your profile. Your username is listed after the final slash of the URL that makes up your online Instagram address.

❖ **Instagram Profile**

Your Instagram profile is where you tell people who you are, and what you like to post. When you click on the option "Edit your profile," you can add your name as the heading of your bio and write whatever else about yourself you would like. You can add a link to another website, such as your social media profile on Twitter or Facebook. At the top of your profile, you can add a picture that will appear at the top of your posts next to your username, and next to any comments you post.

You can find your profile by choosing the person tab at the bottom right of the main screen. On your profile page, you'll find all of the photos and videos you've shared, a map to view your posts based on location and any photos other users have tagged you in (called "Photos of You").

Public: This privacy setting means that anyone can view your posts, the photos people have tagged you in, and your photo map, even if they aren't following you.

Private account: When you activate the private account setting, people who aren't following you can still find and see your profile (bio and user name), but won't have access to your posts, photo map, or photos of you.

Post: Posts are the photos and videos you choose to share on Instagram. To create a post, select the camera tab and choose a photo or video from your phone's library or take one with the app. Then edit the photo and add filters if you want. Next, add a caption, and then share it.

- ❖ **Hashtag**

Hashtags are used to find and give context to your post or comment. For example, if you shared a post about cameras, you could use the hashtags #camera or #technology. Hashtags help other users discover your posts when they search on Instagram. You can find posts with hashtags by searching in the Explore section or clicking any hashtag in the caption of a post.

- ❖ **Photo map**

When you post a photo or video, you can choose "Add to Photo Map" to show your location. If you choose, you can also name your location. That way, your followers or anyone who views your profile can choose your photo map tab to see exactly where you were when you posted specific pictures.

- ❖ **Tagging**

This term has two meanings. The first is when you post a picture that someone appears in or was present for. You can choose the "tag people" option to do this.

The other meaning of tagging is when you comment on a photo or video, and you want to address one or more users directly. To do this, you write your comment and then write @ with their username following it.

❖ **Direct post**

Instagram Direct lets you send pictures or videos privately to up to 15 people. On the home screen in the top right corner, there is an inbox symbol. When you tap the symbol, the screen shows direct posts that you have sent or received. You can go back to a direct post at any time unless the sender deletes it. To send a new direct post, tap the plus sign in the top right corner, or choose the camera tab and go to the direct setting after you have chosen your picture.

Instagram Explore

The Explore tab, represented by a magnifying glass lets you see recommended or trending posts and accounts. When you choose to search, your recent search history pops up, including the hashtags you use most often. The People tab allows you to search for other users by username or full name. The Tags tab allows you to search for posts with a particular hashtag. The Places tab lets you look up posts made in various locations.

❖ **Follow**

When someone follows you, your posts become part of their news feed (the home tab). If you make your account private, the person has to send you a follow request, which you can either accept or deny. If someone follows you, then they can see you in the "following" section of their activity tab, and also see posts you have recently liked or commented on.

❖ **News feed**

The news feed consists of the most recent posts of the users you follow. Every time you log into Instagram, you'll see your feed.

❖ **Like**

If you enjoy another person's post—maybe it's cute, funny, or something you agree with—you can show it by liking it. You do this by double-tapping the post, or by tapping the heart under the person's post.

❖ Block

If you don't want someone to have access to your pictures or look up your account, block them by going to their profile, tapping the menu button (three dots), and selecting Block User.

❖ Activity feed

This tab is shown by a speech bubble with a heart in it. There are two parts to the activity feed: Following and You. The You section tells you if anyone has followed you or has put in a request to follow you, tagged you in a post or comment, commented on your posts, or liked your posts. The Following section shows the recent activity of users you follow, including pictures they've liked and other users they've followed.

❖ Comment

To comment on someone's post, press the speech bubble under the post, write your comment, and then submit it. Keep in mind that comments are not anonymous, and people can report comments as inappropriate.

How To Get Started On Instagram

Start off on Instagram by getting the free app from the Apple App Store or Google Play. When you first open the app, you'll need to register by giving your email, creating a username and selecting a strong password.

Choosing a username and profile picture that represents you is important, but you can change both at any time. For your bio, think about your target audience, whether it's close friends or potential clients or customers, and write something that tells them what they can expect in your posts.

Follow accounts like yours, as well as your friends and family, to connect with others and acquire followers. If you want to follow a celebrity but aren't sure if a particular account is the real deal, look for a symbol of verification next to their name in their bio, if there is no verification symbol, the account may not be verified yet, or the account may be created by a fan.

- **Make Your Account Interesting**

When you start to post, choose things that are flattering, interesting, and relevant. You can edit your photos and videos on the app before you post them using Instagram's filters and easy-to-use tools. Use them to make your photos and videos pop. Make sure to add a caption and a few hashtags related to your account and posts so that others will see your photos and videos.

That should be enough to get you started. Start snapping photos, uploading, and following others to fully enjoy all Instagram has to offer.

INSTAGRAM HANDLE

Instagram is one of the most popular social platforms.

When you create a profile on this social network, you will have to come up with your Instagram handle. But what is a handle, and how does it work? Most people use it every day without wondering what the deal is.

An Instagram handle is something like a phone number. It's a unique link to your Instagram profile. You are the only person with that specific handle. If someone wants to find your profile and follow you directly, you only have to let them know your handle.

Basically, it's your online Instagram address that works like a phone number, but instead of making calls, you can use Instagram's chat and other features to communicate with users.

When creating a new profile on Instagram, you will have to specify a unique handle, or address for others to see. It is an essential step during profile creation, and it can be anything you want, as long as it's not already taken. The handle can be completely different than your real name, or the name of your company.

For example, if your name is John Love, you can call yourself JohnnyLooVe or come up with something that doesn't have anything to do with your name, or occupation. It's entirely up to you, but know that you can only do it once. So, it's vital that you choose the right handle.

INSTAGRAM HANDLE FOR BUSINESSES

If you are a business owner, it's critical that your Instagram handle is as close to the name of your business as possible. Conducting business on Instagram is easy and beneficial in the sense that you can reach a massive audience by using hashtags.

If you own a car dealership, for example, your Instagram handle should probably be the name of your dealership. If the handle is already taken, try changing it without altering the meaning, such as adding auto or car dealership after the name. Once you've come up with a name that represents your company the right way, you will need to use the right hashtags to reach the targeted audience.

- **INSTAGRAM HANDLE FOR PERSONAL USE**

When creating an Instagram profile for personal use, the handle isn't as important. You can use your alter ego, the name of your cat, or whatever else comes to mind, there are no restrictions.

However, if you're looking to become an Influencer, you might want to come up with something catchy, or something that will define your future work. The handle is important because it could attract new followers on its own. If you choose the wrong handle, people could ignore you entirely.

- **CREATING INSTAGRAM HANDLE TIPS**

OK, so, if you want to make use of your Instagram profile, there are a lot of things to consider. You need to find a handle that relates to as many people as possible while still being unique and memorable.

If you're hitting a wall trying to come up with a catchy handle, there are ways that can help you figure out the perfect address for your needs.

TIP 1 – KEEP IT SIMPLE

The Instagram handle has a 30-character limit, so you need to sum up everything you offer into a precise, catchy, and available name. That's often easier said than done. If that's the case with your handle, try doing some keyword research first.

TIP 2 – KEYWORD RESEARCH

Look for keywords used by your competitors and search for them on Instagram. Use the profiles with the largest following as an example and try mixing a keyword with your name, or the name of your company. Strong keywords are usually all taken by now, which means that you'll probably have to go through a trial and error process until you find one that's available.

TIP 3 – USERNAME GENERATORS

After doing some keyword research and failing to come up with one, a Username generator might be the solution you need.

You can find many such services for free on Google. Most of them will ask you to enter a couple of keywords and some other information to come up with an available handle. Here is an example created by Username Generator.

Creating, your unique Instagram, handle could define your success on this social network platform. It's a small, but critical step towards building a large following. So, take your time and try combining the keywords that define your services or type of content.

Choosing a handle can be a little tricky, so take your time and don't rush things.

THINGS YOU NEED TO DO WHEN GETTING STARTED ON INSTAGRAM

- **Download the app**

Instagram is different from other social networks in that it is primarily a mobile platform.

Once your account is set up, you will have a page that can be viewed on a desktop, but the majority of your activity will take place within the mobile app.

Click here to download the app on your phone's app store.

- **Choose a recognizable username**

You can sign up for Instagram with an email address or a personal Facebook account.

Once you sign up, you'll be asked to choose a username.

Your username will display publicly and will be what people see when they find you on Instagram. Make sure the username you choose is recognizable and is as close to your business or organization's name as possible.

When signing up, Instagram will also ask for your full name. Here, you can put your full business name, which will make it easier for people to find you through Instagram's search function.

- **Update your profile**

Instagram lets you fill out a 150 character bio about your business. Because of the text limitations, you'll want to be clear and concise about who you are as a brand and what you offer. If you serve a local customer base, you'll also want to add your location.

Constant Contact uses the bio to share our mission, and let people know what types of photos we share from our Instagram account:

You can also add your business's website, which users will be able to click to visit right from their mobile device.

- **Add a recognizable profile picture**

The perfect Instagram profile photo will be 400×400 pixels.

But what's most important is that the photo you choose is recognizable to people who know your business. In most cases, the best choice will be your business's logo.

Your profile photo can only be updated on a mobile device. If you don't have your logo saved to your smartphone or tablet, Instagram has the option to import it from Facebook or Twitter.

You can also take a new photo with Instagram.

- **Research**

It might not sound fun, but without having a good understanding of the type of pictures others are posting, you won't know what content tends to do well. And lucky for you, Instagram research is less staring-at-piles-of-data-wearing-a-lab-coat kind of research and more look-at-pretty-pictures kind of research.

Start by finding a business in your industry who has a hefty Instagram following, similar target audience, and high levels of engagement. What do they tend to send, and when do they tend to send it?

Even if you want to differentiate yourself from the competition, it's essential that you know what others are doing.

- **Post your first photo**

Okay, now that your profile is set up, it's time to take your first photo.

Here's a quick run-through of how Instagram works:

First, click the icon on the bottom in the middle of the screen.

You can either take a photo by pressing the circle in the middle of the screen, or click "library" on the bottom left to upload a photo of your own.

Note: "Video" on the right enables you to take a video up to a minute.

If you're uploading a photo, you will have the option to crop it first. After that, you'll have options for different enhancements.

You can choose from a number of filters that scroll across the bottom of the app. (Double tap the filter to add a border, or alter the strength of the filter).

You can also click "edit" to access a number of other photo editing features.

Once you're happy with your photo hit NEXT in the top right of the screen. Here, you'll be able to add a caption and hashtags.

You can also tag people and name the location.

- **Setting up your location**

When you click "Add Location," you will see a list of previously used locations in your general area.

If you have a brick and mortar location, you may see that someone has already named your location. If your store, restaurant, or office hasn't been named, you can name it yourself.

After your photo is posted, you will see the location name in blue. When you click on your location name, you'll be able to see every photo that has been tagged there. This can be a great resource for seeing what people like, and want to share about your business.

- **Tell people you're on Instagram**

Leverage, your existing channels to let people, know your business is on Instagram.

If you have an email list, you can send an announcement and ask readers to follow you. Constant Contact integrates with Instagram, so that you can easily upload your Instagram images to your email marketing account.

New to email marketing? Try Constant Contact for free! Sign up for your 60-day free trial.

- **Follow others**

Instagram's search function makes it easy to find people and brands to follow.

You can search by username, or choose relevant hashtags for your business.

Following more people and businesses is a great way to make new connections and can also provide inspiration for your Instagram account.

- **Get social**

You've set up your account, learned the basics, and found the right people to follow; now you're ready to start building a presence for your business on Instagram.

A key component of building an audience on Instagram is engaging with the people who follow you. When someone likes or comments on your photo, you will receive a notification.

You can respond within the comments of a photo by including the "@" symbol, followed by their username.

You will also receive notifications when someone tags you in a photo. You can view all of the photos you've been tagged in on your Instagram profile.

THE INSTAGRAM DO'S AND DON'TS

- DO: ENGAGE WITH YOUR FOLLOWERS!

While social media may be a place for you to express yourself, it's also a place for you to interact with friends, family, fans, etc. Let your followers know they're heard. Give them a like, follow, comment, anything to show you care.

- DON'T: FOLLOW AND UNFOLLOW AND FOLLOW AGAIN AND UNFOLLOW AGAIN

Who doesn't love a new follower? But there's nothing worse than the haunting follow/unfollow cycle until you get a follow back. Just follow, and let the Instagram course take its ride.

- DO: TAG!

It's a great way to engage with other brands and people. Plus, we all want to know where you got those super cute shoes, and we don't really want to ask. There are two types of tagging to be aware of – tagging accounts in the actual photo versus tagging accounts in the caption. There are pros to both. Tagging in the caption displays the account name without people having to click to show tags, giving immediate exposure. However, tagging the account in the photo adds it to their profile's tagged photo section, allowing people who follow them to see it even if they don't follow you. It also makes it more likely the account you're tagging will see the photo even if they're not logged into their Instagram at that moment. If you're working with a brand or professional, make sure you find out if they have specifications for tagging!

- DON'T: TAKE A SPONSORED POST TO TAKE A SPONSORED POST.

More now than ever, our social media has become a reflection of not only who we are, but how we conduct our lives – what brands we use, what people we hang out with, and what we want the world to know about us. Taking a sponsored post for the sake of being #sponsored can cheapen your brand, whether it be a personal or a professional one.

- DO: HAVE FUN WITH IT.

At the end of the day, your social media should be fun! Nobody lives a perfect life, and even though Instagram may be the highlights, we all want to know you're human from time to time. Be relatable; it'll make your content all the more appealing to your followers.

- DO: TAKE ADVANTAGE OF INSTAGRAM STORIES AND INSTAGRAM LIVE!

With Instagram rolling out new features all the time, Instagram stories are a great way to pop up on people's feeds that don't follow you, but probably should. Also, this is a great alternative to giving your followers a peek into your everyday life, without ruining your awesome Instagram feed.

INSTAGRAM FOR BUSINESS

Instagram has proven a worthwhile investment for marketing purposes. You're able to market your products to a more targeted and engaged audience, and it's cheaper than more traditional forms of paid advertising.

Plus, it's an undeniably powerful tool to spread brand awareness -- in fact, 70% of Instagram users have reported looking up a brand on the platform.

But using Instagram for business purposes can seem daunting, particularly if you've only ever used it for personal use.

Step 1: Get an Instagram business account

If you already have a personal Instagram account with brand-appropriate content and an established following, you might want to convert it to an Instagram business account. This gives you access to all the business features, but makes the transition seamless for your existing followers.

You could also choose to create a brand-new Instagram business account. This is the right choice if you don't have an existing personal account, or if your personal account does not accurately represent your business.

- **How To Set Up An Instagram Business Account From Scratch**

Download the Instagram app for iOS, Android, or Windows.

Open the app and tap Sign Up.

Enter your email address and tap "Next." If you want to connect your Instagram business account to your Facebook Business Page, make sure to use an admin email address to sign up, or tap Log in with Facebook.

Choose your username and password and fill in your profile information. (We'll dive into how to optimize your Instagram business profile information later in this post).

Tap Done.

You now have a personal Instagram account that's ready to convert to a business account. Continue by following the steps below.

- How To Convert A Personal Instagram Account To A Business Account

Log into your existing personal Instagram account on the app.

Tap the profile icon to go to your profile.

Tap the three lines icon at the top right of the screen, and then tap Settings.

Tap Switch to Business Profile, and then Continue.

(Optional) If you want to connect your Instagram business account to your Facebook business page, follow the prompts to do so.

Add contact information: Your Instagram for business account must include an email address, a phone number, or a physical address (or all of these).

Tap Done.

Step 2: Create a winning Instagram strategy

Define your target audience

Before you can decide what content to post in Instagram, you need to think about who's going to see it.

The vast majority of Instagram users are under the age of 35, with a reasonably close split between male and female users. The United States has the largest number of Instagram users, closely followed by India, Brazil, and Indonesia. That's good information to get you started, but you need to go beyond these overall Instagram demographics to define a target audience unique to your brand.

Since defining your target market is one of the most important parts of your marketing strategy for any marketing tool, we've created a step-by-step guide that explains all the details. Here's the short version:

Determine who already buys from you.

Check the analytics on your other social media channels to learn who follows you.

Do some thorough competitor research.

Create a clear value statement for your brand.

Once you understand who your audience is, think about what content they want to see from you. What content do they post on their accounts? How do they interact with your competitors or similar brands?

- **Set goals and objectives**

Knowing what you want to accomplish by using Instagram for business is the first stage in creating an effective Instagram strategy. Understanding your goals keeps you on track and allows you to focus all of your efforts on achieving real business objectives.

Effective goals follow the SMART framework. That means they are:

Specific

Measurable

Attainable

Relevant, and

Timely

As you build your Instagram presence, it's okay to have goals based on vanity metrics like likes, follows, and comments. But, make sure you also set goals that relate to real business objectives. This leads us to...

- **Focus on the right performance metrics**

The exact metrics to measure and track will vary for each business. But, broadly, you should focus on metrics related to the social funnel.

That means your goals should align to one of the four stages in the customer journey:

Awareness: Includes metrics like brand awareness, follower growth rate, and post reach.

Engagement: Includes metrics like engagement rate (based on likes), and amplification rate (based on shares).

Conversion: In addition to conversion rate, this includes metrics like click-through rate and bounce rate. If you're using paid ads, conversion metrics also include cost per click and CPM.

Customer: These metrics are based on actions customers take, like providing testimonials.

- **Commit to a regular posting schedule**

Once you start building a following on Instagram, your fans will expect to see posts from you regularly. You want to keep them aware of your brand and engaged with your content without overwhelming them to the point that they tune out—or worse, unfollow.

There's no one time that's best to post for all businesses. Hootsuite and Unmetric analyzed 200,000 Instagram posts in 11 different industries, and determined that the best time to post on Instagram varies greatly depending on your industry. The Food and Beverage industry, for example, finds the most success posting at noon, while the Education industry receives lost of engagement when they post at 4 p.m.

Besides benchmarking your account against other top brands in your industry, you'll need to do some testing to determine what times seem to create the most engagement for your posts (more on that later).

The key factor is to understand when your audience is online. Remember that they may not be in the same time zone as you are. Instagram Insights shows you exactly when your followers are online, broken down by day.

To access this information, go to your Instagram business profile, click the three bars icon in the top right, then click Insights. Click on the Audience tab and scroll down to see active times.

Once you determine your best time to post, create a content calendar to plan and schedule your Instagram content in advance.

Step 3: Optimize your profile

You entered some basic profile information when you first created your Instagram business account. Now, it's time to optimize your profile for the best results. Here's a quick video that goes over the highlights:

- **Tweak your bio**

Your Instagram bio is only 150 characters long, but it needs to do a lot of heavy lifting. It tells first-time visitors who you are, what your brand is all about, and why they should care.

How do you cram so much information into such a small space while also conveying brand personality? We've got a full guide to creating an effective Instagram bio for business, but here are some quick tips:

Use your brand voice: Convey your personality. Go casual, or professional, or a little bit cheeky, depending on what makes the sense for your business.

Include hashtags: Instagram bio hashtags are clickable, and are a great way to show off user-generated content.

Try emoji: These little symbols can help you convey a lot of information in just one character.

Use spacing and line breaks: Line breaks make your bio easier to read online.

- **Optimize your profile pic**

For most businesses, the best profile pic is some version of your logo. Use the same picture you use on other social profiles to help people instantly identify your brand.

Your profile photo displays as 110 x 110 pixels, but it's stored at 320 x 320 pixels. That means it's a good idea to upload a photo, at least, 320 pixels square to ensure you're ready if Instagram changes how profile photos are displayed.

Your profile pic is cropped into a photo on the app. So, make sure your logo is fully visible in this shape.

- **Make sure your profile is complete**

Use all the components of your Instagram business account to their full advantage.

Name and username: These are the only parts of your Instagram profile that are included in Instagram search, so use them wisely. Include your real brand name, as well as any variations (like a common abbreviation). By using the same username (or handle) on all social networks makes it easier for fans to find you.

Website: This is the only spot on Instagram where you can post an organic clickable link, so be sure to include one! Link to your website, your latest blog post, a current campaign, or a special Instagram landing page.

- **Take advantage of Instagram business profile features**

When you use Instagram for business, you gain access to several profile features not available to personal accounts. Whether you're converting a personal account or starting from scratch, make sure you take advantage of these business-only options:

Contact information: Include your email address, phone number, or physical address so fans can connect with you directly from your profile. When you add contact information, Instagram creates corresponding buttons (Call, Email, or Get Directions) for your profile.

Category: This appears under your name and shows people at a glance exacly what you do.

Call-to-action buttons: These allow users to book an appointment, make reservations, buy tickets, and more, right from your Instagram profile. From your business profile, tap Edit Profile, then Contact Options, then Add an action button.

Comme Deux uses all of the available business profile options for the Instagram business account. Their physical address is shown, the category is indicated as Health/Beauty, and they have a Shop call-to-action button.

Step 4: Share great content

Create a visual aesthetic for your brand

Instagram is all about the visuals, so it's important to have a recognizable visual identity.

First, think about what you will showcase in your posts. In some cases, the content will be obvious: a clothing line might showcase its clothes, and a restaurant might post photos of its food.

If you offer services, try showcasing customer stories (maybe gathered through a branded hashtag). Or go behind the scenes to highlight office life, or introduce fans to the people who make your company tick.

Once you decide on a content theme, then go for a consistent visual look. That means consistent colors and filters, and an overall aesthetic that is easy to spot as your fans scroll through their Instagram feed.

Chef and author Dennis Prescott has a visual style that's instantly recognizable, and they get an incredible engagement rate. With less than half a million followers, he routinely racks up 10,000 to 20,000 likes and hundreds of comments on his posts.

- **Take amazing photos**

To make Instagram work for your business, you've got to have great photos. But you don't need to be a professional photographer, and you don't need a lot of equipment.

Your mobile phone is your best friend when it comes to Instagram photography, since you can post straight from your device. Here are some tips to get the best photos when shooting with your phone:

Use natural light. No one looks great with a flash lighting up the oiliest parts of their face and casting weird shadows on their nose and chin. The same is true for product shots. Natural light makes shadows softer, colors richer, and photos nicer to look at.

Avoid harsh light. Late afternoon is an unbeatable time to take photos. Cloudy days are better than sunny ones for mid-day shooting.

Use the rule of thirds. Your phone camera has a grid built in to help you follow this rule. Place your subject where the grid lines meet to create an interesting photo that's off center, but still balanced.

Try different angles. Crouch down, stand on a chair–do whatever it takes to get the most exciting version of your shot (as long as it's safe to do so, of course).

- **Edit your photos like a pro**

No matter how great your photos are, you'll likely want to edit them before posting to Instagram. Consistent editing is one way to maintain your brand aesthetic, and make your images recognizable.

Mobile photo editing apps like VSCOcam or Enhance provide additional filters or editing options to help you find your unique style. You can import photos that you edit or filter elsewhere into Instagram to post them on your feed.

- **Tell great stories with Instagram Stories**

More than 400 million people use Instagram Stories every day, and 39 percent of people surveyed said they became more interested in a product or brand after seeing it on Stories. A third of the most viewed Instagram Stories are posted by businesses.

Content that disappears after 24 hours and live broadcasting features make Instagram Stories the perfect place to take creative risks with attention-grabbing photos and videos.

How can you make the most of Instagram Stories? Not surprisingly, this aptly name feature is a great platform for storytelling. Tell authentic brand stories that have a beginning, a middle, and an end. Get creative with Stories slideshows and provide real value for your viewers to get them in the habit of watching your Stories consistently.

End your Stories with a powerful call-to-action to convert your Stories views into measurable business successes.

Need some inspiration? Check out some great examples of brands using Instagram Stories effectively.

Want to extend the life of your Instagram Stories content beyond 24 hours? You can do that with Instagram Stories Highlights.

- **Write compelling captions**

Instagram may a visual platform, but that doesn't mean you can neglect your captions. Captions allow you to tell the story that makes the photo meaningful. Captions can make your followers think, laugh, and feel a connection to your brand.

To create compelling captions, you need to develop a clear brand voice. The most important thing is to be consistent. Do you use emoji in your captions? Are there grammatical guidelines your brand follows? What hashtags do you use? A good set of style guidelines will help keep your captions distinct and on-brand.

For tons of great Instagram caption examples, and tools that will help you make your captions even better, check out our post on how to write Instagram captions for business.

Step 5: Grow and engage your audience

- **Follow and engage with relevant Instagrammers**

Social networks are all about community. A community relevant to your brand already exists on Instagram. You just have to find them. One way to do that is to engage with people and brands they already follow.

Start by monitoring industry hashtags and commenting on appropriate Instagram posts.

Follow the people who participate in these discussions. This is a simple way to make your presence known to people who are likely to be interested in your content.

As you get more involved in Instagram communities, you'll get a sense of the hashtags that inspire the most response.

- **Hashtags help make your Instagram content easier to find.**

Captions on Instagram are not searchable, but hashtags are. When someone clicks on or searches for a hashtag, they see all the associated content. It's a great way to get your content in front of people who don't already follow you.

You might want to consider creating your branded hashtag. A branded hashtag embodies your brand and encourages followers to share photos that fit that image. It can be a great source of user-generated content, and encourage community among your fans.

Amsterdam Marketing uses the #iamsterdam hashtag to collect user-generated content, which they reshare to promote a colorful and visitor-created feed of the city.

- **Respond to comments and mentions**

Remember: this is social marketing. You can't neglect the social aspect. That means responding to comments and mentions of your brand on Instagram, so users feel motivated to keep engaging with your brand.

You might be tempted to automate your engagement using bots. Don't do it. We tried it, and it doesn't work out so well. Dedicate some time to responding authentically when someone mentions or tags your brand.

- **Work with Instagram influencers**

Influencer marketing is a powerful way of gaining access to an engaged and loyal Instagram following by working with an Influencer whose fans might be interested in your brand.

Even small brands with limited budgets can use influencer marketing by working with micro-influencers: people with a smaller but dedicated following.

For real-world insights on how to best work with Instagram influencers to grow your Instagram business following, check out our insider tips in this post from influencer Lee Vosburgh, creator of the 10×10 Style Challenge.

- **Promote your account on other channels**

If you've got an established following on other social networks, let those people know about your Instagram business account. Make sure to tell them what content you'll share on your Instagram profile, so they know why it's worth their time to follow you in more than one place.

Include your Instagram handle in your email signature, and don't forget about print materials like business cards, flyers, and event signage.

- **Use Instagram ads to get in front of a large and targeted audience**

Instagram can provide great organic business results, but it's also worth investing in Instagram ads to ensure you get your content in front of a wider (but very targeted) audience.

In addition to extending the reach of your content, Instagram ads include call-to-action buttons that allow users to take action straight from Instagram, reducing the number of steps required to get them to your website or promotion.

- **Run an Instagram-specific campaign**

An Instagram campaign can help you achieve a specific goal more quickly than you could by simply following your overall Instagram business marketing strategy.

Campaigns can involve ads, but they're not only about paid content. They involve intense focus on a specific goal for a set period of time, in both your organic and paid posts.

We walk you through all of the details in our post on creating successful Instagram marketing campaigns, but here are some potential campaign ideas to get you started.

Run an awareness campaign to increase your overall visibility on Instagram.

Promote a sale using shoppable Instagram posts.

Drive engagement with an Instagram contest.

Collect user-generated content with a branded hashtag.

Step 6: Measure success and make adjustments

- **Track results with analytics tools**

Once you're using Instagram to promote your business, you need to check-in regularly to see how your progress matches up to your business goals.

You'll want to track the results of individual posts, ads, and stories, as well as your Instagram business account as a whole.

There are a lot of numbers to keep an eye on, but there are plenty of analytics tools to help you keep it all sorted.

We've got the details in our post on the seven best analytics tools when using Instagram for business.

- **Use A/B testing to learn what works (and what doesn't)**

One of the best ways to consistently improve your results is to test each new strategy to see how it performs. As you learn what works best for your specific audience, refine your strategy.

Here's the basic outline of an A/B test on Instagram:

Choose an element to test (image, caption, hashtags, etc.)

Create two variations based what your research tells you. Keep the two versions the same except for the one element you want to test.

- **Track and analyze the results of each post.**

Choose the winning variation.

Test another small variation to see if you can improve your results further.

Share what you learn throughout your organization to build a library of best practices for your brand.

Start the process over again.

And there you have it—now, you're ready to craft your strategy and put it into action. Good luck.

REASONS TO USE INSTAGRAM FOR YOUR BUSINESS

Since its inception, Instagram has proven to be a powerful marketing tool for businesses looking to expand their presence and the visibility of their products. If you have not jumped on the Instagram bandwagon yet, you may be doing your business a great disservice. If you still need convincing, then check out these reasons why Instagram is continuously rising in importance, and how your company can benefit.

- ❖ **More people are using Instagram.**

According to the folks at Instagram, their social media presence currently brings with it over 800 million active users. Of those millions of people, over 500 million are on the platform daily, with 80 percent of them being outside of the United States, 34 percent of them being millennials and 38 percent checking the site multiple times each day. With that many available eyeballs, there is no limit to the success a business can reach with a dedicated Instagram strategy.

- **Any size of business can thrive.**

With all of those users to choose from, the sky is the limit to what a business can achieve. That goes for large, well-known companies, as well as smaller mom and pop shops, and one-man operations.

Of course, even for the best-known companies, success will not come overnight, but if a marketing team wants to get their organization on the map, they can do so by keeping an active presence and maintaining a routine of, at least, one post per day. This is how both household names like Coca-Cola and Adidas, as well as a slew of small businesses have effectively used Instagram to thrive.

- **Businesses can make money directly from Instagram.**

Instagram has evolved over the years, and now, there is a greater emphasis on making money through product placement. The latest program is called shoppable posts, and they allow businesses to add tags to the products in their photos with links that include a product description, price, and the ability to "shop now," which will lead the user to your online store.

With this new service, it's simple for a business to attract actual sales from the site, and with 72 percent of Instagram users admitting to purchasing products through the social media platform, the results are hard to ignore.

- ❖ **Stories make your business relatable.**

Instagram is a great way to show potential customers that you are more than just a faceless corporation. This can be done through many of the app's features, but you can make an impression with live posts and stories.

The best way to use live stories is to show behind-the-scenes insights into your company and the people who work there. Some examples are videos that show how products are made, videos of office employees interacting with each other, and live Q&A sessions between you and your audience.

Instagram live posts are also an excellent way to build rapport, trust, and credibility with followers, as well as showing that there's a human side to your business. If consumers see you as more than an entity looking to take their money, then they may be more trusting of your brand.

❖ **You can partner with influencers.**

When it comes to social media, you have your regular viewers, and then you have influencers. For those not in the know, influencers are online celebrities who will often promote a brand or product and take it into the mainstream.

A dependable influencer can bring your company's sales to a whole other level through increased return on investment and access to demographics that you wouldn't normally reach. If you use a well-known influencer, then they can spread word of your company or product to millions of followers with just a few posts.

❖ **Hashtags can increase your visibility.**

As a new business on the block, you may be intimidated by the competition, but with the proper use of hashtags, you can separate your company from the herd.

Hashtags are essentially keywords that summarize what your post is saying. Popular Instagram hashtags such as Coca-Cola's #ShareaCoke, Charmin's #TweetFromTheSeat and Calvin Klein's

#MyCalvins have rocked the industry, becoming pop culture cornerstones that have made these popular companies even more recognizable and beloved.

You may not be Coke or Charmin, but effective use of hashtags can do wonders to separate your business from the crowd.

❖ **You can effectively engage with customers.**

What is better than having customers know you exist? How about the opportunity to engage with them on a daily basis? The fact is that people like to make their opinions known, especially if they like something, and Instagram is a platform for users to like, comment on and share their favorite posts. The more likes and comments you get, the more visible your company becomes. You can get more likes by taking high-quality photos, using local hashtags and partnering with other brands.

❖ **Mobility is king.**

Unlike Facebook and Twitter, which started out as browser-based sites, Instagram was created to be an app from the start. Since 90 percent of time spent on mobile is spent on apps, your company should take advantage of this and make your posts accessible to viewers wherever they go via Instagram. Smartphone users tend to turn to Instagram because it has a cleaner style than the cluttered view that Facebook can create, and with engagement on Instagram being ten times higher than on Facebook, you will want to get on the bandwagon.

❖ **You can keep an eye on competitors.**

Your company can use Instagram to keep an eye on your competitors and see how they interact with their followers. Watch carefully to find out how often they post, what they are posting and how they engage with their followers. You can use the information you gather to better define your own personal strategy.

❖ **It offers many ways to get creative.**

A great benefit of the photo-sharing app is the creativity it provides. On Instagram, your marketing team can go wild coming up with new ways to draw attention and add followers and new customers. Show the public that your brand has personality, and that it is cool to shop with you by mixing it up with contests, shoutouts, vivid images, interactive videos and more.

If anything ties these benefits together, it is that more people are paying attention to Instagram than ever before, and you are only ignoring millions of potential customers by not joining this powerful social media platform. Take the tips you learned here, and use them to start building your Instagram presence. Your bottom line will be glad that you did.

BENEFITS OF OPERATING AN INSTAGRAM BUSINESS PROFILE

Access to Instagram Insights

Instagram provides little in analytics and performance statistics for the average Instagram user. This used to be a problem for businesses, so they created Instagram Insights for businesses and power users.

Instagram Insights provides businesses all of the essential data they need to know about their account, and how their posts perform. It helps provide insight into what content works and what doesn't. It gives you information about your followers to help you build a picture of those who take an interest in you.

It shows you your performance on Instagram over the last week - change in followers, number of posts, impressions, reach, profile views, website clicks, and email clicks.

It then gives you detailed demographics of your followers – their gender, ages, locations by cities and countries, and when they are most active.

Instagram Insight also lets you a view your historical posts by engagement and impressions over a period you set up to two years.

Of course, there are times when you may want even more detailed analytics about your Instagram performance — we have previously looked at Top Instagram Analytics Tools and Software Solutions.

Ability to Add a Contact Button

A useful addition permitted for accounts with a Business Profile is the ability to add a Contact button to your profile. When somebody clicks on the button, you can set so that they can email you, dial a telephone call with you, or provide them with a map showing your location.

Your Industry Will Show on Your Profile

When you created your Facebook page, you were asked to select the industry in which your business operates. So, when you then connect your Instagram Business Profile to your Facebook page, this information crosses to your Instagram profile. You can modify this information directly within Instagram if you need to in the future.

Ability to Add Links to Instagram Stories

One of the most annoying thing about Instagram, from a marketing point of view, is that you generally can't use clickable links. If you operate a personal profile, the only link, you could use is one in your profile.

Instagram Stories provides another option, however. We recently described How to Use Instagram Stories Like an Expert. One useful option for some Instagram accounts is the ability to add a URL to your Instagram story.

This is particularly valuable when, as reported by Locowise, 75% of Instagram users take an action such as visiting a website after looking at a post.

The ability to add links to Instagram Stories isn't available to all businesses, however. You need to have a business profile with 10,000 followers before Instagram gives you access to this feature.

Able to Advertise on Instagram and Make Promoted Posts

If you have the budget to promote your Instagram posts and advertise on the platform, you will need to operate a Business Profile.

This is another area where the connection between Facebook and Instagram is obvious. You build your ads on Facebook and choose where you want your ad placed. Instagram is one of the options Facebook gives you – the others are various positions on Facebook and Messenger.

TIPS FOR MASTERING INSTAGRAM FOR BUSINESS

❖ **Show what you do in a creative way**

Focus on the solution you provide, and not the products you sell. On Instagram, it's essential to add value to your customers and look pretty while you do it. Never underestimate the fact that your most important asset (and downfall) on this social media network is visual content.

If your business is service-oriented, focus on showcasing the process behind providing the service. Show your company culture, share your mission with the world, or share some tips and how-to.' It's possible to upload photos, short videos (similar to GIFs, called Boomerangs), and videos up to one minute in length.

❖ **Try Instagram Stories**

Instagram Stories have a slideshow format and are only live for 24-hours (though they can be saved to your device to be re-used later). This new feature is a direct competitor to Snapchat's Stories, and is now being heavily developed by Instagram. These are some of the benefits of using Instagram Stories for brands:

Stories are prominently displayed at the top of follower timelines under the Instagram logo.

It can be used to capture behind-the-scenes content that doesn't have to be as high in quality as regular posts.

Makes it easy to experiment with different content types: photo, short video, Boomerang (GIF-like image), video filmed backward (Rewind) and live video.

Tagging other accounts, e.g. @instagram in Stories is ideal for collaborators and influencer marketing.

Fun additions like face filters, text, and stickers help you edit images on-the-go.

Story search for hashtags and locations make them more discoverable.

All photos and videos you add will play in the sequence they were added and you can add as many as you like. Instagram Stories adverts became available to all businesses globally in March 2017. You can use these to target new audiences and add CTAs to your collages which can be especially useful for promotions. Check out

Single Grain's ultimate guide to running Instagram Stories Ads for a full step-by-step guide to creating your first one.

Note that Stories are only available on the mobile app, and it's possible to send Instagram Stories as a direct message (DM). The use of social media Stories is definitely picking up and almost any brand can find fun and engaging way how to participate.

❖ 2. Create a winning profile

As a company, you probably do a whole lot of things and offer even more solutions. Don't get too caught up in fitting all of that in 150 characters. Focus on your most important USP or your next big thing - be it an event, promotion or product launch.

Since the only clickable link is in your Bio section (right under your name), make a habit of updating it frequently. It's a shame that most brands use it only to link to their website, but it could do so much more. Think, driving event registrations, app downloads or even purchases.

Instagram has also launched their Instagram Business profiles and paid advertising. The Business profile adds a phone number to your bio and gives access to extensive analytics data that wouldn't be otherwise available unless you're using a social media tool. Read our blog on how to set up an Instagram account for business where we walk through you the step-by-step instructions and key elements you need to consider when managing Instagram for other businesses.

❖ **Take them behind-the-scenes**

Customers have a natural curiosity about where their products come from, and you can use Instagram to show them their whole lifecycle. This is, especially relevant for companies that sell environmentally friendly or FairTrade products. Source images to demonstrate how products are made - from the base material, production, and distribution.

If nothing comes to mind, you can share something that everyone has - sketches, notes, and filled whiteboards, or blackboards. Every business has brainstormed ideas, it's up to you to take a pretty picture and upload it to Instagram. You may find that it's best to try out different post types until you strike gold with the one that will engage the audience. Thanks to yet another new feature, Instagram now lets you archive posts instead of deleting them.

❖ Expand your reach with #hashtags

Use hashtags to expand your reach. These can be campaign specific or general - all that's important is that they are relevant. Make sure to also set up your main company hashtag (#yourbrandname), and use it sparingly across Instagram (Twitter is good too). This makes it easier for people to find content related to you, as well as your main account.

It's best practice to use between three to five hashtags, despite the fact that the maximum you can add is 30 per Instagram post. Use your campaign specific hashtags, as well as the more popular hashtags to increase the discoverability of your content. For example, try adding hashtags like #instagood (used is 300 million posts), or #tbt (Throwback Thursday), and don't forget about industry-specific ones. If you are in IT, the hashtag #IT or #tech will do just fine. Also, consider how you add hashtags, these can be added at the end of the post, in a comment or worked into the actual post, like GoPro does.

❖ Collaborate and @mention others

Instagram is one of the strongest social media channels for highlighting collaborators and sharing customer success stories. Even if you don't officially partner with a non-profit organization, you can give to charity or do a fundraiser a couple of times a year. It's all good as long as the cause aligns with your brand values and mission. Take into account that not everyone is monitoring hashtags on social media, so tagging an account is usually a better choice if you want to get noticed.

Another technique involves the use of 'shout-outs.' An unpaid shout-out is when you partner with another brand that has roughly the same number of followers as you to promote each other to your audiences and you both benefit from increased exposure.

The paid shout-out is for those with a bigger budget as it's essentially an influencer campaign. This usually involves paying a brand (or influencer) with a much larger following to promote your product or service. It's a great way to gain a large number of new followers quickly, providing that you create a strong call to action and the influencer's audience is genuine.

- ❖ **Build anticipation and offer exclusivity**

Keeping your customers interested is an essential part of any effective marketing campaign. Reward your loyal followers with exclusive content. Let them be the first to know about new products, services, or events. Create teaser photos that build anticipation or satisfy curiosity for your new releases, office openings, or stores. This preview makes your Instagram followers feel special and keeps them coming back for more insider information.

- ❖ **Analyze your success and build on it**

Without taking a step back and analyzing what worked and didn't, marketing becomes a guessing game. The truth is, you can read all the articles in the world about the best practices and publishing times, but you will only find out what works for your clients through testing and measuring results.

Social media management tools can help, though. You can use them not only to schedule your Instagram campaigns in advance but also use social media analytics to measure their success. Make sure to regularly measure your follower count, engagement and clicks, all to refine and improve your strategy. Our new social media reports can help you track your performance for Instagram and all other key social media networks.

HOW TO CREATE AN INSTAGRAM BUSINESS PROFILE

Creating an Instagram business profile is simple! By following these easy steps, you'll be well on your way to adding a new tool in your social media marketing toolbox.

- **Download the Instagram app**

While Instagram is accessible through the computer, you'll need to download the app on your mobile device to create an account to gain full access to all of the brand's features. If you have a designated smartphone for your social media marketing efforts, use that! If not, consider using the personal phone of your social media marketing professional or whoever will be spearheading your Instagram strategy.

Grab your smartphone, search for Instagram in the app store, and download! The visual below will give you a good idea of what to expect. As a heads up, we'll be using iPhone screenshots throughout this post. However, the Instagram app is also available on Android.

- **Create a non-business Instagram account**

The next step is to create your Instagram account. If you've created a personal Instagram account in the past, this should be a familiar process! You don't switch your account to a business profile until after it's almost entirely complete.

Instagram will prompt you to sign in with your Facebook account. While this may seem like a shortcut, we do not recommend linking your profiles. If you do, Instagram will create your account based on information from your personal Facebook.

Instead, create an Instagram account using the business email of whoever will be running the Instagram profile. You may also consider creating a dummy email for all of your social media profiles, like socialmedia@companyname.com.

- **Selecting your username and password**

Once you create your Instagram account, you'll get to start making the profile your own. Based on the name you signed up with, Instagram will suggest a username for your account. If you entered your company's name initially, you may choose to keep the suggested Instagram handle. If you entered your name initially, or the name of the person who will be running the Instagram account, you'd want to change the username to your company name.

This step is easy. Press the "change username" button. In almost all situations in social media marketing, your social media username should be the name of your company and consistent across all platforms. This will make it easy for your customers to find you and increase brand affinity when you start posting pictures and videos.

You'll also select a password at this stage. Don't forget that multiple marketers on your team may need to access the Instagram account, so avoid making your password the name of that goldfish you had when you were nine.

Instead, select a password that is secure and business related – not one that you'd be embarrassed to share with your chief marketing officer if they ever asked.

- **Find accounts to follow (or skip this step)**

The next screen you see will prompt you to find people to follow through Facebook and within your contacts. While you can complete this step if you'd like, we recommend waiting until your profile is more complete before you begin following other brands or individuals.

There's a chance that those you follow will follow you back, so consider holding off until you've posted some content and built out your profile more. You'll always be able to go back and find contacts through Facebook, so hit "skip" (at the very bottom of the screen) for now, and know you can take advantage of this feature later.

Find accounts to follow (or skip)

- **Uploading a profile picture for your account**

Now, it's time to upload a profile picture! When it comes to social media marketing, a primary goal is to increase brand affinity. Users should visit your profile and immediately know just what company they're looking at. An easy way to ensure this happens is by using your logo as your profile picture.

While social media's casual nature may make it appealing to use, a group picture or something a bit more "out-of-the-box," remember that this is a business account and not your personal page. That doesn't mean you can't use the pictures eventually! Just save those fun shots for your actual posts. Using your logo as your profile picture will help your followers relate the stellar content you post back to your brand.

- **Switch to an Instagram business account profile**

At this point, you'll switch your Instagram profile to a business profile! As a disclaimer, this requires you to have a Facebook business page.

If you do have a Facebook business page, then this process is even easier. At the top right corner of the page, open the settings menu. This button is a gear in iOS, or an ellipsis on Android phones.

From there, you'll scroll down until you see the option to "Try Instagram Business Tools." Select this, then click through the slideshow until you're prompted to connect your Instagram to your Facebook business page.

At this point, Instagram will ask for permission to manage your Facebook page. Select "yes" – this enables Instagram to link to your Facebook business page. Once you complete this step, you're all set! Your Instagram profile is now a business profile, and you have access to the valuable insights the app offers.

- **Complete your Instagram business profile**

Now that you've successfully turned your Instagram profile into a business profile, you can start building it out with some information about your organization and brand.

Before you start posting pictures and videos, you'll want to fill out your Instagram bio and contact information fields. This will ensure that anybody visiting your profile has an idea of what you do, where you're located, and how they can contact your team.

To do this, tap on the profile button on the bottom right to see your account. This button is a picture of your profile picture, so it'll be easy to find! Click the "edit profile" button that sits at the top of your page.

This is where you can update your page bio and contact information fields. Keep in mind that your Instagram bio is limited to 150 characters. Briefly summarizing what you do should be more than enough information! Don't worry if you're not feeling inspired just yet – you can come back and edit this section whenever you'd like.

You'll also add your contact information and website. This is the only place on Instagram that you can put a clickable URL (unless you're a business account with more than 10,000 followers), so take advantage of the opportunity and link to your primary website. And, don't forget to set up your Instagram Nametag and display it in your business. This makes it easy for customers to find your new business account on Instagram.

Complete your profile

- **Start filling your business account with valuable content**

Congratulations! Your Instagram business profile is complete. It's time to start filling your page with the exciting content your audience seeks. To upload a photo or video press the plus sign button that sits at the bottom of the page. From there, you'll be able to select the photo you want from the phone's gallery.

Once you're well-versed in taking, editing, and posting Instagram pictures, you can start exploring Instagram stories and the various other opportunities the app offers!

Start sharing posts

Utilizing your new Instagram business account

Now that you have all the tools you need to build your Instagram business profile, it's time to explore the opportunities that come along with it!

DOS AND DON'TS OF INSTAGRAM MARKETING

Crafting an effective Instagram marketing strategy is still super puzzling to a lot of industry professionals. You read that right: even those whose job it is are often just winging it. And with good reason: it's a brand new trade that doesn't yet have any career veterans. In fact, those who currently work in the field of social media marketing are primarily writing the playbook.

A little-known fact is that the titles of social media manager, social media editor, and community manager don't mean the same thing in every company. Because there is no standard mold, there are no firm guidelines for these roles, and every business will characterize tasks differently. To make matters even more convoluted, practices that work wonders for one brand — like say, using the best hashtags available or the practice of video marketing — may fall flat for the next.

And because this is a vital activity for every modern business, it needs to not be. If you work in social media, chances are you've hit a wall more than once. Whether your drawbacks were related to issues with Instagram etiquette, strategy, daily operations, or chaotic work flow situations, know that you are not alone. Social marketers, even the best ones, hit these kinds of snags more often than you think.

To help solve your most pressing issues, we've put together a comprehensive list of Instagram marketing tips in a very direct dos and don'ts format.

- **PROBLEM: Low Engagement**

DON'T: Use Bots

DO: Focus on Community

Slow it down right there, cowboy. We can understand how frustrating it can be if your account's engagement is lagging. But don't do anything regrettable out of sheer panic, like using Instagram bots to boost your visibility and trigger exchanges. Not only is it cheating, but it's not a cute look. For anyone.

Putting a band-aid on the problem is not going to solve anything, and it feels counterintuitive when there's a more sustainable and valuable long-term solution. Say it with me: COMMUNITY. We're high preachers of this Instagram concept, mostly because we've witnessed it being core to social success on many occasions.

If you want your engagement to go up, you're going to want to reevaluate how you approach community-building, audience interactions, and the use of Insta hashtags. Followers don't engage with brands they don't care about. If you don't show them any love, or don't act like you're in it for them, and you will get nothing back. The best way to promote your Instagram account is by having your community do it for you (cough, Glossier, cough). Here are some easy steps: first, build. Second, foster. Third, give back. Fourth, manage.

- **PROBLEM: Few Sales Conversions**

DON'T: Start Being Aggressively Salesy

DO: Take advantage of all hyperlink placements and adjust your content and CTAs

Sure, Instagram is mainly used for product discovery versus as a shopping platform, but that doesn't discard it form the revenue race. For your account to drive sales conversions, you first need to make sure that your audience is engaged (see point above). Then, you must make the most of what is available to you.

If you have Insta's native shopping functionality, make sure you test out and adjust your call-to-action. But also utilize every single spot (aka opportunity) to link out of the app and onto product pages, or any other relevant URL that you think, would bring value to your followers.

For example, the ever so efficient link-in-bio solution (Dash Hudson's LikeShop) can help drive new revenue through Instagram on top of driving growth. The numbers speak for themselves. Pro tip: always make sure you test out various CTAs to see what works best for your brand, and link to the type of content that your audience responds most positively to. The more you engage, the likelier you are to successfully make conversions.

Yet another area where you can maximize your traffic and sales opps is in Instagram Stories. A lot of brands forget that if they have a business account with over 10k followers, they can capitalize on immediacy in Stories by inserting a link to enable discovery or purchase. Do a lead up, and then insert your link. Make your people feel like they're missing out if they don't swipe up. Increase traffic. Drive conversions. It's a well worth it process.

Instagram marketing tips for business, Instagram do's and don'ts, instagram best practices 2018, using instagram for marketing, Topshop instagram stories content strategy

Topshop is inserting links where it counts to maximize every conversion opportunity.

- **PROBLEM: Stumped Growth**

DON'T: Buy Followers

DO: Be Introspective

There comes a time in every life cycle when dreaded staleness sets in. Nothing is immune to this phenom, especially the incredibly fast-paced world of social media that never stops evolving. In fact, I promise that if you do a quick competitor analysis, you'll find that you are far from alone.

That said, if your growth rate has slowed, the last thing you should do is to buy followers to inflate your number. Just like using bots (see point #1), it's not a cute look. First, of all, this practice is so obvious to anyone who surfs the Insta waves on the daily (read: all of humanity), and your disingenuousness will be transparent. Fake is lame, period.

Now that we've settled that, if something has changed, you need understand why and how to remedy to it. It could mean that a transition is happening. It could also indicate that the algorithm has been revised and that you have to find fresh ways to navigate its new settings, here is your set-by-step guide to figuring things out.

- **PROBLEM: Low Visibility**

DON'T: Start Spamming People

DO: Place a Few Well-Crafted Ads

Advertising on Instagram used to be a bit of a taboo, we know. But not anymore, as more brands and influencers are using ads more freely than in the past. In fact, it's a marketing trend on the up and up. While Insta doesn't have Facebook's full on pay-for-play model, it still offers businesses the ability to shell out for exposure if they're not happy with what they're getting for free.

Next time you're hoping to get more eyeballs on your posts, the best and easiest way to do so is through boosting. But don't just push out a promo and call it a day. Do the research to understand how to approach the practice to be able to craft an effective content and caption strategy. Then start testing and see what sticks. There is no magic formula, but once you find what works, the Insta world will be your oyster.

- **PROBLEM: No Street Cred**

DON'T: Fake It Till You Make It

DO: Hire Influencers

Listen, not everyone can be a Reformation, we get it. It's especially brutal if you're just starting out and trying to hustle. Building Insta street cred is a tough feat that requires patience, but you want to accelerate things a little bit, we get it. There are two words you need to familiarize yourself with: influencer marketing.

Align yourself with popular on-brand (v important!) Instagrammers so that their cool image rubs off on your business while they simultaneously spread the good word about it. A novel idea, isn't it? There's a reason for why influencer marketing works.

Decide on an approach, build a strategy, go about sourcing efficiently, and learn more about the benefits of using micro-influencers to determine if that angle is right for you. Either way, it's going to lend your brand credibility and, if executed properly, a campaign can put you on the map. If you have the budget, this one is a no-brainer.

Every single one of these points is intertwined and has a ripple effect on the bigger picture — the success of your activities at large relies on all of your output. Remember to always be (reasonably) critical of how you're executing to constantly evaluate what you could improve upon.

Make sure that your content is up to snuff, that you're using all available tools that you're properly abreast of the competition, that you have the bandwidth to sustain constant efforts, and that you devise both a short-term and a long-term strategy to reach your goals.

STEPS TO EFFECTIVELY USE INSTAGRAM TO GENERATE SALES

Almost every brand understands that Instagram is a great marketing tool. However, more than half of brands do not know how to leverage Instagram. A shocking statistics showed that more than 60% of small businesses in Toronto have never used Instagram to generate any type of sales.

With this amount of users, your audience is definitely on Instagram whether you sell cars or cow dung, someone on Instagram is waiting to buy what you are selling.

The problem is that most small business owners don't have a clue how to use Instagram to generate sales. Some of these people know that Instagram has the power to bring additional sales but lack the necessary knowledge to make it happen. These people also consider themselves unable to hire professional social media managers due to small marketing budget.

However, any investment in Instagram marketing definitely worth it. If you cannot afford to hire an Instagram marketing manager, the least you can do is to learn how to make use of Instagram marketing to generate sales. You can definitely do it if you are willing to put in some efforts.

When you create a business account on Instagram; you will be able to add additional contact information that isn't available for personal profiles. This information includes your website, business phone number, and address. You will also be able to leverage Instagram analytic tools to know how you are performing on Instagram.

Using Instagram for marketing will help you create more awareness, boost brand visibility, reach a wider audience, and generate more revenue. In this article, you will learn of ways you can easily make use of Instagram marketing to generate more sales.

Ways To Make Use of Instagram To Generate Sales

Build Your Followers

It is a simple logic – if you want more followers on Instagram, you need to have more followers. You cannot generate as many sales as you want if you don't grow your audience. The more followers you have, the more potential customers you will be able to reach.

Of course, you cannot go out there and get just anybody as followers. You need to ensure that your followers are people that are a good fit for your business. When you are starting out on Instagram marketing, a lot of social media managers will approach you to give you fake followers, don't fall for this.

Naturally build your followers. Use engaging contents to target people that might be interested in your business. You can partner with a social media influencer to make this process faster. Once you increase the number of your followers, not only you can sell to them, but you can turn them into your advertisers.

Engage Your Instagram Followers

Honestly, this is harder than it sounds. You need to come up daily with posts that interest and engage your followers. Make sure you are adding values to your followers if you want them to trust you.

When you are just starting out, forget about selling and focus on building trust. You can start by creating a bio that stands out. Keep your bio short and sweet, highlight exactly what you offer, and create a direct CTA using a memorable URL.

When you are done, make use of quality contents, user-generated contents, contests, polls, discounts, promo codes, stories, Instagram stories, and much more to keep your Instagram followers engaged. Keep on posting educational posts. Post at least three times a week so remain fresh on your followers' mind. You need to add value to your followers in order to get their trust.

Turn Your Followers Into Customers

Now is the most important step. However, this is easy if you have done step two perfectly. When your followers see you as an authority in the industry, it will be extremely easy to sell to them.

To generate sales using Instagram marketing, you will need to come up with posts that will trigger an emotional reaction. You may have the best product in the world, but you won't make a sale if you don't show it in a way that brings about interest and stirs up emotion.

The best way you can do this is to make use of creative design and visually stunning imagery. Make sure that your product can solve your audience's problems. Your post about your product needs to be exciting and it needs to generate an emotional response. You should add a direct link to the product or tell your followers exactly how to get the product. You can attract additional sales with Instagram ads or when you work with an Instagram influencer.

Use creative, relevant hashtags.

Use a service like #TagsForLikes to help generate a list of the most popular, on-topic hashtags for each of your posts. If you aren't using the right hashtags, you're missing out on a huge opportunity to be discovered by potential customers and other people interested in the things you're posting about!

Find your Instagram "voice.

"In business blogging, it was all about developing a brand voice. Now, in this highly visual new world, you need to find your company's unique Instagram style. I wrote an article recently about companies that are killing it on Instagram, and Audi was one of the brands I featured, thanks to its distinct image style. Adding your logo won't cut it (and will turn people off)--your branding has to be defined by your image composition, colors, topical relevance, and more. It's worth investing in getting your Instagram style right.

Final Words

You can generate tons of sales on Instagram if you do your marketing right. With the tips above, I believe you now have a clue about how Instagram marketing works. Remember to track your success to know that you are doing right, and where you need to improve. Overall, be consistent – this is what makes the difference between a successful Instagram marketer and a failed one.

INSTAGRAM HACKS

General Instagram hacks

- ❖ **Stop seeing posts and/or Stories from specific accounts you follow**

Mute annoying users without the risk of offending them with an unfollow.

How to do it:

Tap the icon in the corner of a post from the account you want to mute

Click mute

From there, you can choose whether to mute posts, or mute posts and Stories from the account

You can also mute posts and Stories by pressing and holding on a Story in your tray, or from a profile

- ❖ **Rearrange the order of your filters**

Put your most-used filters up front for faster posting.

How to do it:

When posting a photo or video, go to Filter

Scroll to the end of your filters and tap Manage

Press and hold the three line icon next to each filter on the left-hand side of the screen to rearrange the order of your filters

Check or uncheck the circles next to each filter on the right-hand side of the screen to hide or unhide filters

Click Done to save your settings

❖ **See all the posts you've liked**

Looking for inspiration? Why not review what's already inspired you.

How to do it:

Go to your profile

Open the hamburger menu in the top right corner

Tap Settings

Tap Account

Tap Posts You've Liked

❖ Clear your search history

Don't let anyone who has access to your phone know how obsessed you are with your frenemies.

How to do it:

Go to your profile

Open the hamburger menu in the top right corner

Tap Settings

Scroll to the bottom, and then tap Clear Search History

❖ Hide specific search queries

Permanently remove specific searches (accounts, hashtags, places, etc.) from appearing in the search bar.

How to do it:

Tap the magnifying glass icon to visit the search page

Tap the search bar at the top of the screen

Tap the X to delete

deleting users from search results Instagram

❖ Get notifications when your favorite users post new content

Never miss a post from your favorite people and brands!

How to do it:

Visit the profile page of the account you'd like to get notifications for

Tap the three dots icon in the upper right-hand corner of the screen

Select Turn on Post Notifications

Note: If you've changed your mind, the option to turn off notifications lives in the same spot.

❖ Add and manage multiple accounts

You can add up to 5 accounts under the same email address on Instagram. And you don't need to log in and out to switch between accounts.

How to do it:

Go to your profile and tap the hamburger menu.

Tap Settings.

Scroll to the bottom and tap Add Account.

Enter the username and password of the account you'd like to add.

To switch between accounts you've added:

Go to your profile.

Tap your username at the top of the screen.

Tap the account you'd like to switch to.

switching between multiple accounts Instagram

❖ Pin your Instagram post to Pinterest

Pinterest isn't listed as one of the network choices when sharing a post from Instagram, but there are workarounds for both Instagram mobile and desktop.

How to do it on mobile:

Go to the post you'd like to Pin

Tap the three dots icon located above your post to the right

Select Copy Share URL to copy the post link to your clipboard

Open the Pinterest app on your mobile device

Tap on your profile image icon to visit your profile

Tap the plus sign icon at the top right of the screen to add a new Pin

An "Add a board or Pin" menu will appear, select Copied link

Pinterest will automatically open the link saved to your clipboard

Choose the image you'd like to Pin and finish posting as usual

How to do it on desktop:

Visit Instagram.com and find the post you'd like to Pin

Right-click on the post and select Open Link in New Window

Use the Pinterest browser button to choose the image you'd like to Pin and finish posting as usual

❖ Delete comments

Whether you need to hide an offensive comment or erase a typo, deleting comments is easy.

How to delete your own comment:

Tap the speech bubble icon beneath the post you commented on

Find the comment you'd like to delete

Swipe to the left over the comment

Tap the trash can icon

How to delete another user's comment on your post:

Tap the speech bubble icon beneath the post containing the comment you'd like to delete

Swipe to the left over the comment

A partial swipe will bring up a trio of options, allowing you to reply, flag, or delete a comment

Tap the trash can icon—or continue swiping to the left—to delete the comment

❖ **Filter and block comments based on keywords**

Dealing with a social media troll? Comment controls allow you to filter and block comments containing specific keywords.

How to do it:

Go to your profile and tap the hamburger menu.

Tap Settings.

Tap Privacy and Security.

Tap Comment Controls.

Make sure that Hide Offensive Comments is turned on.

Tap next to Manual Filter to turn it on.

Enter specific words, phrases, numbers or emoji in the text box to filter out comments.

When you turn on comment filtering, it's applied to both new and existing comments on your posts.

When you turn off comment filtering, filtered comments on your posts will be restored.

❖ Turn off comments on a particular post

How to do it:

Begin posting a photo or video as usual

When you reach the screen where you add a caption, location, and other tags, select Advanced Settings

Toggle the Turn Off Commenting option on

turn off Instagram comments

Note: you can change this setting even after a post has been published by going to the post, tapping the three dot icon above it, and selecting Turn On Commenting. You can also turn off comments on a previously published post by following these same steps.

❖ **Reply to comments faster**

Do your followers ask a lot of the same questions? For example: "When will this be back in stock?" or "What are your holiday hours?"

A handy hack exists for iOS users that will help you reply to these questions quickly and efficiently.

How to do it:

On your Instagram profile, tap the hamburger menu, and then Settings.

Tap General, and then Keyboard.

Tap Text Replacement.

Here, you'll see a list of pre-populated keyboard shortcuts. Click the + sign in the upper right corner.

In the Phrase section, type the generic response you would like to create (e.g., "Hi! We're open from 9 am to 3 pm on Memorial Day.).

In the Shortcut section, type a word or abbreviation that will represent that full phrase, like "MemorialDay."

Anytime you want to use that specific comment, type out your shortcut and your phone will automatically populate the full phrase.

❖ Save and organize posts where only you can see them

The perfect hack for squirreling away bits of inspiration. Or use this feature to keep tabs on your competitors.

How to do it:

Go to a post you'd like to save

Tap the bookmark icon underneath the post you want to save

Add the post to an existing collection or tap the + icon to create and name a new one

To see your saved posts and collections, visit your profile and tap the hamburger menu. Then tap Saved.

organize Instagram posts

❖ Remove old posts from your profile without deleting them

This is possible thanks to Instagram's archive feature.

How to do it:

Tap ... at the top of the post you want to remove

Select Archive

Tap the Archive icon in the top right corner of your profile to review all archived posts

If you want to restore content to your public profile, tap Show on Profile at any time and it'll show up in its original spot

❖ Zoom in on a post

How to do it:

Go to the post you'd like to zoom in on

Pinch using two fingers and slowing the pull them farther apart

Enjoy the details

❖ **View how much time you've spent on Instagram**

How to do it:

Go to your profile and tap the hamburger menu.

Tap Your Activity

Instagram settings Activity screen on Instagram

❖ **Set a reminder to limit your time on Instagram**

Only want to spend a certain amount of time on Instagram per day? Set a reminder to let you know when your time is up.

How to do it:

Go to your profile and tap the hamburger menu.

Tap Settings.

Tap Account > Your Activity > Set Daily Reminder.

Choose an amount of time and tap Set Reminder.

❖ **Customize which notifications you receive**

Want to only receive certain types of notifications? Or pause them all together. It's easy to do that.

How to do it:

Go to your profile and tap the hamburger menu.

Tap Your Activity.

Tap Notification Settings.

Click into each notification category to opt out of specific notifications. Go to Pause All and toggle on to pause all notifications.

Instagram hacks for photo and video sharing

❖ **Make your captions more readable with line breaks**

If you favor the long-form caption a la National Geographic, this hack would make your posts more readable.

How to do it:

Edit your photo and proceed to the caption screen

Write your caption

To access the Return key, tap the 123 key on your device's keyboard

Use Return to add breaks to your caption

Note: The breaks will start a new line, but not create the white space that you would see between two paragraphs. If you want a paragraph break, write out your caption in a note app and copy it to Instagram. To break up lines further, consider using punctuation, such as bullet points or dashes, to hold the place of an empty line.

❖ **Use individual photos to make a larger one**

Get creative and have fun with Instagram's grid format.

How to do it:

To share a #triplegram, simple share three related images consecutively so that they take up an entire line with a single unified look

To share a grid post series, try cropping a single image into nine (apps like these can make the process easy) and share them in quick succession

❖ **Adjust the intensity of filters**

For those who want something close to—but not quite—the #nofilter look.

How to do it:

After uploading or taking a photo, tap the filter you'd like to use

Tap the filter again to open edit options

Use the sliding scale to adjust the intensity of the filter

Tap Done to add the filter to your post and continue your edits

❖ **Upload or capture a post with multiple scenes**

It's an Instagram Story that never disappears!

How to upload a post with multiple photos and video clips:

Tap the + icon in the navigation bar at the bottom of the screen

Tap SELECT MULTIPLE on the Library tab

Choose the photos and videos from your camera roll that you want to include in your Story

Choose and edit your filters (you can choose a different filter for each photo or video or make it consistent across the entire post)

Once you've selected your videos, you can tap to trim them or press and hold to reorder

To delete a clip, drag it to the center of the screen

Finish your edits as usual and share your masterpiece

How to record a video with multiple clips:

Tap the + icon at the bottom of the screen

Tap Video

Tap the circle icon to begin recording

To take multiple clips, lift your finger off the circle icon to pause, then press and hold it when you want to begin recording again

To delete a previous clip in your video, tap Delete, then tap again to confirm

❖ Share videos without sound

If the audio is bad and/or doesn't add to the viewing experience, you may as well remove so it's not a distraction.

How to do it:

Tap the + icon at the bottom of the screen to select the video you'd like to upload

Tap Next

Tap the volume control icon at the top of the screen to mute the video's sound

Note: This can also be done in Instagram Stories. After recording a video, simply tap the volume control icon at the top of the screen to mute.

❖ Save drafts for later

You've snapped the perfect shot and edited it to perfection, but the perfect caption eludes you. Save the post as a draft—with all your edits intact—and come back to it later.

How to do it:

Tap the + icon at the bottom of the screen to shoot or upload a photo or video

Edit the post as you like, adding filters, captions, tags, or a location

Hit the < icon in the upper left-hand corner of the screen to go back to the editing screen

Hit the < icon again

A pop-up menu will appear, select Save Draft

When you're ready to continue with your edits and share your post, tap the + icon, then select Library

A new DRAFTS section will now appear above CAMERA ROLL

Tap your desired post, or select Manage to view all of your saved drafts

Select a post, edit, and share as usual

Save drafts in Instagram

Note: To delete a post from your saved posts, select Manage to go to Drafts, then tap Edit. Select the posts you'd like to get rid of and tap Discard Posts at the bottom of the screen, then tap again to confirm.

- ❖ **Blur the background on a portrait photo**

How to do it:

Open the camera and select Focus among the options under the record button

Take a selfie or switch to the rear-facing camera to snap a photo of someone else

The subject will stay in focus while the background blurs

Blurred portrait photo Instagram

Note: this feature is only available on select Android devices, iPhone SE, 6S, 6S+, 7, 7+, 8, 8+, and X.

- ❖ **Request to join another user's Live video (or encourage followers to join yours)**

Brands can use this feature when partnering with other businesses or influencers for announcements, Instagram takeovers, and the like. Or, encourage your followers to join a live Q&A you're hosting.

How to request to join a live video:

When watching a live video, tap Request in the comments section

You'll see a confirmation when the user accepts and you'll have a moment to prepare

Once you're live, the screen will split in half

You can leave the live video at any time

How to accept a request from a follower to join your live video:

When hosting your live video, you'll see a notification for each request in the comments section

Tap View and then choose to add the requestor or cancel the request

The icon with two smiley faces will have a red number showing how many requests you have

Tap the icon, and you'll see both requests and current viewers

You can either accept a request or invite any viewer to join you. You can remove a guest and add someone else at any time

❖ **Save your live video**

How to do it:

After your live broadcast ends, tap Save in the upper right corner

After saving, tap Done and your live video will be saved to your camera roll but will no longer be available in the app

❖ **Record video hands-free**

How to do it:

Swipe right from your home screen to open the Instagram Stories camera

Swipe through the options at the bottom of the screen—normal, Boomerang, etc.—and stop at the HANDS-FREE recording option

Tap the record button at the bottom of the screen to begin recording

To stop recording, either let the maximum time run out, or tap the capture button again recording hands free

- ❖ **Add as much text as you want to posts in Stories**

How to do it:

Swipe right from your home screen to go to the Instagram Stories camera

Snap an image or record a video

Tap the screen to add text OR tap the Aa icon in the upper right-hand corner

Write your desired text

Tap the > icon

Repeat as many times as needed to add more text

- ❖ **Change the color of individual letters, or words in your text**

How to do it:

Swipe right from your home screen to go to the Instagram Stories camera

Snap an image or record a video

Tap the screen to add text OR tap the Aa icon in the upper right-hand corner

Write your text as usual

Press and hold on a word or individual letter to select and highlight

Choose your desired color

Continue editing and share as usual

❖ **Change the colors or info displayed on a sticker**

How to do it:

Select a sticker to add to your post

Tap it for different color options, or, in the case of things like the temperature sticker, you can choose between Celsius and Fahrenheit

❖ **Share someone else's post in your feed on Instagram Stories**

The Instagram Story version of a regram—great for sharing user-generated content or giving a shoutout to another relevant brand or influencer.

How to do it:

Click on the paper airplane icon below the post you want to share

Tap Add post to your story

The post will appear as a sticker with a custom background

You can rotate, scale, move the sticker, and tap it to explore other styles

Once you're happy with how it looks, tap the Your Story button to add it to your post. The post will show original poster's username. When someone taps the post, they'll be able to see the original post and more content from the person who created it.

Note: You can only share posts from public accounts. If you don't want your posts shared on Instagram Stories by other people, you can opt out in settings.

❖ **Add a soundtrack to your Story with Instagram's music library**
There are thousands of songs to choose from!

Once you taken a photo or video to add to your Story, tap the Stickers icon (folded smiley face) at the top of the screen

Then tap the MUSIC sticker from the menu to open Instagram's music library

Choose your song by searching for a specific track or browse by mood, genre, or what's trending

Tap play to preview the song before adding it to your Story

Once you've selected a song, you can fast-forward or rewind it to start it at a specific point

Finish adding to your post as usual and click the Your Story button at the bottom to publish it

❖ **Share a song or album from Spotify on Instagram Stories**

Show off how hip your brand is.

How to do it:

Open the Spotify app

Find the song or album you want to share

Tap the three dots to open the options menu

Scroll down and tap Share

Tap Instagram Stories

This will open the Instagram app and you can add a sticker, text, or doodle to the image of the album you're sharing (if you're sharing a specific song, the app will still display the album it's on)

Then tap Your Story to add the song

❖ **Get music recommendations with the questions sticker**

Whether you want fresh music to get in the holiday mood, or new tunes to get you through the last few weeks of school, your friends can now help you find the perfect tracks.

How to do it:

Tap the square happy face on your Story to Add a questions sticker.

Tap the questions sticker and then tap the music icon to let people send you a song. People can tap the sticker in your Story, then type a question to ask you or send you a song.

When you view your own story and swipe up, you can see who responded. Tap a response from someone to share it. Their photo and username won't be shown.

❖ **Save your entire Story to your camera roll**

In case you want to publish it on a different channel later.

How to do it:

Open your Story

Swipe up on the screen

Tap the arrow in a circle icon in the top right corner of the screen

Note: You can also save individual posts from your Story as you upload them by tapping the downward arrow icon in the bottom left corner of the screen. If you've already shared it, go to the photo or video you'd like to save, tap the three dots icon in the bottom right corner, and select Save Photo.

❖ **Share your Story to your profile**

If your Story's hot and you want everyone to see it—even those who don't login during the 24 hours that it's live—publish it on your profile.

How to do it:

Open your Story

Tap the three dots icon in the bottom right corner of the photo or video you'd like to share

Tap Share as Post

Edit—add filters, tags, a caption, etc.—and post as you normally would

❖ Find out how your Story's performing

Want to know how your Story's doing? Check out this little-known feature to find out who's watched it.

How to do it:

Open your Story

Swipe up on the screen

Instagram will display the number of views as well as the names of people who have seen each photo or video in your Story

❖ **Zoom in and out on videos with a single finger**

How to do it:

Swipe right to open the Instagram Stories camera

Hold down the capture button with one finger to begin recording video

Slide up or down with the same finger to zoom in or out

❖ **Hide your Story from specific users**

How to do it:

Method 1

Go to your profile and tap the hamburger menu.

Tap Settings.

Tap Privacy and Security > Story Controls.

Tap Hide Story From.

Select the people you'd like to hide your story from, and then tap Done (iOS) or the checkmark symbol (Android).

To unhide your story from someone, tap the blue checkmark to unselect them.

Method 2

You can also choose people to hide your story from as you're looking at who's seen your story.

Tap the three horizontal dots (iOS) or the three vertical dots (Android) to the right of their name and select Hide Story From [Username].

Note: Hiding your story from someone is different from blocking them, and doesn't prevent them from seeing your profile and posts.

❖ Hide your Story from a location or hashtag

How to do it:

Tap Seen by on your Story.

Viewers who are seeing your story via a location or hashtag page will appear at the top.

Tap x to the right of a location or hashtag page to hide your story from it.

❖ **Only share your Story with close friends**

Make a "close friends list" to share more personal moments with a smaller group that you choose.

How to create a "close friends list":

Go to your profile and tap the hamburger menu

Tap Close Friends

Tap Add next to the people who you want to add to your close friends list. You can also tap Search to search for a friend.

Tap Done when you've finished adding people to your list.

You can update your list and remove people at any time. People won't be notified when you add or remove them from your list.

How to share your Story with close friends:

Tap the camera icon in the top left or swipe right from anywhere in feed.

Tap the circle at the bottom of the screen to take a photo, or tap and hold to record a video. To choose a photo from your phone's library or gallery, swipe up anywhere on the screen.

When you're ready to share, tap Close Friends in the bottom left.

People on your close friends list will know they're on it, but they can't see who else is on your list. If someone has added you to their list, you'll see a green badge when you're viewing their stories and a green ring around their profile photo.

❖ Hide someone's Instagram Stories without unfollowing them

Whatever the reason, we all follow at least one account whose content we may not like but for some reason can't unfollow. The solution? Muting their Instagram Stories.

How to do it:

Tap and hold on the Instagram Stories avatar of the account you'd like to mute.

Tap Mute. This moves the story to the end of the queue and prevents it from autoplaying.

To unmute, just tap and hold on the stories icon and tap Unmute.

❖ Add a text-only post to your Story

A picture says a thousand words, but sometimes you only want to say a few words.

How to do it:

With Instagram Stories open, select Type under the capture button

Tap the screen and write your message

Click the button at the top-middle of the app to cycle through the various styles

Choose a background color and text color(s)

Press the > icon when you're happy with the design to post it to your Story

❖ Share any size photo or video without cutting anything out

Now you can share that wide-angle company photo without cutting out Gary from accounting.

How to do it:

Upload your large photo or video and pinch to zoom out to share the original dimensions

Any extra room will be filled with a custom color gradient that matches what you're sharing

- ❖ **Pin your best Stories to the top of your profile**

Brands can now keep their best Stories on their profiles for as long as they like with the Instagram Stories Highlights feature.

How to do it:

Tap the New circle at the far left on your Instagram for business profile

Choose any Stories from your archive (note: Stories from business profiles are automatically saved to the archive when they expire)

Select a cover icon for your Highlight and give it a name

Your Highlight will appear as a circle on your profile that plays as a stand-alone Story when someone taps it

To edit or remove a Highlight, tap and hold it on your profile

Note: Highlights stay on your profile until you remove them, and you can have as many Highlights as you'd like. Check out these free Highlights cover icons to make sure yours really stand out.

❖ Share your Instagram Story to your Facebook Story

You can do this for individual post, or set it up so all your Instagram Stories automatically our published on Facebook as well.

How to do it for a specific Story:

Start creating a story, then tap Next.

Tap Your Facebook Story.

Tap Share.

How to set up automatic Facebook Story sharing:

Go to your profile and tap the hamburger menu.

Tap Settings.

Tap Privacy and Security > Story Controls.

Next to Share Your Story to Facebook, toggle on to allow sharing.

- ❖ **Share a replay of your live video on Instagram Stories**

Another feature available to business accounts.

How to do it:

When you finish broadcasting a live video, simply tap Share at the bottom of your screen and the video will be added to your Story.

Note: The recording will be available for 24 hours. While it plays, it will display all the comments and likes from the original broadcast. Brands will also be able to see exactly how many people watched the video—both live and in Stories.

❖ **Share a sneak peak of your Instagram Story**

Want to entice your audience to watch the rest of your Instagram Stories? We've got a simple trick for that.

How to do it:

Open Instagram Stories and take a photo, or select one from your library by swiping up.

Tap the pen icon in the upper right-hand corner of the screen.

Select a color.

Tap and hold on your screen for 1-3 seconds until the screen is filled with a solid color.

Tap the eraser symbol in the top right corner.

"Erase" the part of the picture you would like to show by swiping or tapping the screen with your index finger.

Tap Your Story to share the finished product.

❖ **Link to your IGTV video from Instagram Stories**

If you've just started an IGTV account, give your followers an easy way to find your new content—by sharing it to your Instagram Stories.

How to do it:

In Instagram Stories, select the image you would like to post (a screenshot or a still from your IGTV video).

Tap the link icon on the top right-hand side of your screen and select IGTV video from the Add Link menu.

Select the correct video and tap Done in the top right corner of your screen.

Now your followers can go to your IGTV video by swiping up on your Instagram Story.

❖ **Include a hashtag or profile link your bio**

You can now link to a hashtag page or another account in your bio.

How to do it:

Tap the profile icon to go to your profile

Tap Edit Profile and go to the bio section

Type # or @ and then a list of recommended hashtags and accounts will appear

Once you select the hashtags and accounts you want, they will linked to in your bio

Note: When you mention someone else's profile in your bio, they will receive a notification and can choose to remove the link. Their profile will remain in your bio but without a link.

- ❖ **Hide photos you've been tagged in (or remove the tag entirely)**

Has your brand ever been tagged in an image that you'd rather not be associated with? There's ways to remove it from your profile.

How to do it:

Tap the person icon to visit your profile

Tap the person in a box icon beneath your bio to go to the Photos of You tab

Tap the photo you want to remove from your profile

Tap the three dots icon in the upper right-hand corner and select Photo Options

Select Hide from My Profile or Remove Me From Post if you want to untag yourself

Pro Tip: You can also choose whether or not you'd like tagged photos to appear on your profile. To do it, go to the Photos of You page, tap the three dots icon, select Tagging Options, then choose either Add Automatically or Add Manually.

- ❖ **Add line breaks in your bio to make it stand out**

If you'd like to break up the block of text that is your bio, this hack is for you. Line breaks are a great way to include info in a visually appealing way.

How to do it on mobile:

Open up a notes app and write out your bio as you'd like it to appear—line breaks included

Select all the text and choose Copy

Open the Instagram app

Tap your profile image icon to visit your profile

Tap the Edit Profile button

Paste the text from your notes app into the bio field

Tap Done to save your changes

How to do it on desktop:

Visit your Instagram profile on the web

Select Edit Profile

Space your bio as you'd like it to appear

Click Submit to save your changes

Note: Whether edited via mobile or on desktop, profiles viewed on desktop will appear without line breaks.

- ❖ **Include a link in your bio to drive traffic**

Your bio is a great place to drive traffic to your website or another social channel with a link.

How to do it:

Tap your profile image icon to visit your profile

Tap the Edit Profile button

Enter in the link you'd like to share

Tap Done to save your changes

Pro tip: Include UTM parameters in the URL to track how much traffic is generated by the profile link.

❖ **Make your bio appear in more search results**

The name field in your bio is searchable. If you include keywords related to your business in your name, you'll be more likely to appear in the search results of people looking for businesses in your industry.

How to do it:

Tap on Edit Profile on the top right of your Instagram profile

In the Name section, change the text to include your keywords

Tap Done on the top right corner of your screen

❖ Change the alignment of your bio

Tired of the old left screen alignment? There's a way to center—or even right—align your bio.

How to do it:

Go to your Instagram profile in a web browser (it's easier than on mobile).

Copy the space between the arrows (not the arrows themselves!) : >>⠀⠀⠀⠀⠀<<

Tap Edit Your Profile from your profile page on Instagram

In the Bio field, paste the spaces you copied above before each line of text. Add or delete spaces to align further right or left.

Note: You only have 150 characters for an Instagram bio and each "space" counts as a character.

❖ **Add special characters to your bio name or caption**

Some Instagram profiles have special characters like hearts, stars, and pencils in their Instagram bios. You can have them too!

How to do it:

Open a Word or Google doc.

Start typing your bio. To place a special character, tap Insert, then Advanced Symbol.

Add the icons where you would like them in your bio.

Open your Instagram profile in a web browser and tap Edit Profile.

Copy and paste your bio from the Word or Google doc to your Instagram bio and tap Done when you're finished.

❖ **Switch to a business profile to run ads and get analytics**

If you're a brand and still don't have an Instagram business profile, you're missing out on key features and insights. Make the switch now.

How to do it:

Go to your profile and tap the hamburger menu

Tap Settings

Tap Account

Tap Switch to Business Account.

Connect your business account to a Facebook Page that is associated with your business. This will make it easier to use all of the features available for businesses. At this time, only one Facebook Page can be connected to your business account.

Add details such as your business or accounts' category and contact information.

Tap Done.

Find the best (and most relevant) hashtags

Because using the right Instagram hashtag will make your content more discoverable and allow you to grow your audience.

How to do it:

Select the magnifying glass icon to visit the Explore tab

Type in a keyword and tap the Tags column

Choose a hashtag from the list

This will take you to a page of posts bearing that hashtag

Above the "Top" and "Recent" portions of the page, there appears a small bar labeled "Related." Next to this, Instagram will display a list of relevant hashtags that you can swipe through for inspiration (and further research)

❖ **Follow your favorite hashtags**

Great for content inspiration!

How to do it:

Select the magnifying glass icon to visit the Explore tab

Type in the hashtag you want to follow

On the hashtag page click the Follow button

❖ Save hashtags for future use

If you often use the same hashtags for every post, save them in a note to save time.

How to do it:

Create a new note in the notes app on your mobile device

Add all of your most-used captions to a running list

Whenever you're sharing a post, navigate from Instagram to the notes app, copy your text, then paste it in your caption

❖ Hide hashtags on your Instagram posts

Don't clutter your captions. Hide your hashtags to keep the reader focused on what's important.

How to do it—method No. 1:

One easy way to hide your hashtags is to simply leave them out of your caption altogether and put them in a comment below your post

Once you've got another comment, your hashtags will be safely hidden in the comments section

How to do it—method No. 2:

Another method is to separate your hashtags from the rest of your caption by burying them beneath an avalanche of line breaks

Simply tap the 123 key when composing a caption

Select Return

Enter a piece of punctuation (whether a period, bullet, or dash), then hit Return again

Repeat steps 2 to 4 at least five times

Instagram hides captions after three lines, so your hashtags won't be viewable unless your followers tap the more option on your post

❖ Hide Hashtags on your Instagram Stories

You can include up to 10 hashtags on an individual Story, which will significantly increase the number of people who will see it. However, you may not want your Story to look too cluttered. Luckily, there are two easy ways to hide your hashtags and keep your Story looking clean and polished

How to do it, method 1:

After you've typed your hashtags out, shrink them to as small a size as possible using your thumb and index finger.

Place a sticker, large emoji, or GIF over them.

hashtags on an Instagram story hashtags on an Instagram story covered up by a sticker

How to do it, method 2:

After you've typed your hashtags out, shrink them to as small a size as possible using your thumb and index finger.

Tap your hashtags again.

Then tap the ink dropper icon in the bottom left corner.

Tap on the area where you plan to hide your hashtags. This will turn the hashtag text the same color as the background, effectively hiding them from view.

❖ **Turn off your activity status**

If you don't want your followers to know when you were last active on the app, you can turn off activity status within Instagram Direct Messenger.

How to do it:

Tap the profile icon at the bottom right of your screen

Tap Settings

Scroll down and select Activity Status

Toggle off activity status

❖ **Send disappearing content to other accounts**

You can send a disappearing photo, video, or Boomerang to another account or a group of friends using Instagram Direct Messaging.

How to do it:

From the home screen, tap the camera icon at the top left of the screen. Or swipe right to open the camera. Or open Instagram Direct by tapping the paper airplane icon at the top right of the screen, then tapping the camera icon in the top left

Shoot a photo, video, or Boomerang

Edit it as desired

Tap the > icon at the bottom right of the screen

Choose your recipient OR tap New Group to send your message to several people in a single group chat

Tap Send at the bottom of the screen

Note: If you select multiple recipients without creating a group, each user will be sent the same message separately.

❖ Send a live video

You can send your live video or one you're watching to a user or group of users.

How to do it:

When shooting a live video, tap the Direct icon (paper airplane) at the bottom of the screen and send your live video to friends (you'll also have this option when going live with a friend)

Once sent, the recipient will see your live video in their Direct inbox. Friends can only view your video if you're currently live

- ❖ **Edit a friend's photo and send it back to them**

How to do it:

When viewing a photo message from a friend, tap the camera icon at the bottom and capture a reply

Your reply includes a sticker of what you're replying to

Move and resize it, and add your own twist with stickers, text and drawings

INSTAGRAM FOR BUSINESS HACKS

❖ **Use Linktree to drive traffic to your best work**

Linktree is one of the best Instagram hacks

One of the toughest parts of Instagram marketing is that you can't put links in your posts. You only get one place to promote an external website on your entire Instagram presence: in the link box in your bio.

So, make the most of your single link with Linktree. This tool lets you quickly build mobile-friendly micro-websites that link to your best blog posts, products, and merchandise right from your bio link.

❖ **Use location tags for more engagements**

Location tags a crucial part of any Instagram post. Studies show that posts with a location tag get 79% more engagement than those without, meaning that you're giving up valuable engagements and reach by not using them.

This works because—when you add a location tag to a post—it's added to the location's Instagram page. Instagram users can then browse these location tags and find your content in the process.

Post your location tag to broad locations. For example, instead of tagging a specific coffee shop or your office, tag the surrounding area, or neighborhood. Ultimately, this will get your photo in front of people visiting the area and looking for things to do.

So, how do you add a location tag? Simple: tap the Add Location button underneath the caption section when posting to Instagram. You can also add location tags in step ⅗ of the Social Report scheduler.

❖ **Make an Instagram stories playlist**
Instagram recently added the ability to add "story highlights" to your Instagram profile. These highlights look the same as any other Instagram

story, but instead remain on your profile permanently (instead of disappearing in 24 hours).

You can create these by navigating to your Instagram profile and clicking on the plus button underneath the Story Highlights header. You'll be presented with a log of your past Instagram stories content, and you can click and choose which you want to add to your highlight.

Make Instagram story highlights that teach your audience how to do something. Like in the albums example above, you can use this to create tutorials and other how-to content that your audience members will find interesting.

Alternatively, you can use these to show off your best work. For example, if you're a design agency, you may want to use story highlights to show off your best designs and client work.

However you use story highlights though, make sure you're showing off excellent content that boosts your brand image and makes people want to look deeper into your brand.

- **Use shorter captions (because we're all time-poor)**

Do you want people to actually read your captions? Don't try and max out the character limit.

Instead, we highly recommend sticking with short, punchy, and straight-to-the-point captions on Instagram.

This makes your captions easy to read when people are scrolling through their Instagram feeds late at night or on their subway commute to work. And with more people wearing glasses than ever, you'll make your nearsighted followers happy too.

- **Let a user know when you reshare their posts**

Resharing another Instagram account's posts—whether on your feed or your story—can be an excellent way to show some love to accounts you like while expanding your reach at the same time.

After all, if a brand sees you share its best work, chances are they'll give your profile a look and give you a follow too. Oh, and if karma is any indication, maybe they'll even share your posts in the future!

However, when you reshare someone's post, they're not immediately notified that you did it.

Because of this, it's on you to write a "thank you" note of sorts after sharing Instagram content. In this message, give the account a heads up that you shared its post, and tell them to keep up the awesome work.

❖ **Use up to 30 different hashtags (with care)**

Nowadays, Instagram lets you add 30 different hashtags to the captions of your Instagram posts. The benefit to this is—when you add hashtags to your post—your posts become visible in a search for said hashtag.

So if, for example, you're a skateboard company, using hashtags like #skateboards, #skateboarding, and #skatepark would make your posts visible to people searching in those hashtags.

Further, Instagram users can now follow hashtags that they're interested in. When following a specific hashtag, they'll get notifications when there are new posts in said hashtag, making it easier to find new Instagram accounts that post content they're interested in.

Make sure to capitalize on this and consistently use related hashtags in your posts. This will—like mentioned earlier—get your content in front of new eyes that are hungry for the content that you're already posting.

Just note that it's never a good idea to use hashtags that aren't related to your content. This will only make your posts look spammy and serve your posts to people that aren't interested in your content.

❖ Consider running a high-quality photo contest

Sweepstakes and contests are one of the easiest ways to boost your engagement and help you gain followers in a pinch. But instead of hosting a random giveaway, get creative and host a photo contest.

In this contest, have your followers take a photo of your product or of another subject of your choosing. Then, have them post the photo to their Instagram feed, tag your account, and use a giveaway-specific hashtag.

Run the contest for a few weeks and pick your favorite photo as the winner. When all is said and done, you'll have made one of your followers happy, and expanded your network by having your followers post about your products for an entry.

It's truly a win-win for everyone!

❖ Post content at all the right times

Schedule your Instagram posts at the right time

Timing is a super important thing to keep in mind when posting content to your Instagram feed.

Despite the network moving away from a strictly chronological feed, we've found that recently posted content still performs better than older content in terms of ranking at the top of the Instagram timeline—that is, if you're posting when your followers are most likely to check Instagram.

Obviously, though, everyone's followers are different.

Each set of followers logs on at different times, ultimately engaging with content at different times too. Because of this, you'll need to get creative (dare we say "scientific"?) when finding the best times of day to post to Instagram.

One of the best ways of doing this is by looking at historical engagement data. This is when you look at when people have interacted with your content in the past.

However, this can be a tough statistic to find manually. So, with that in mind, we recommend using Social Report's optimization report to find the data and crunch the numbers for you.

In this report, you can view when your followers like your posts within any given reporting period. You can use this historical data to guide when you post to social media, all the way down to the hour.

Additionally, keep your audience in mind when choosing when to post. For example, if you run a local coffeehouse in Brooklyn, chances are you'll want to post before and after New York working hours when people are most likely to check their Instagram feeds.

- ❖ **Likewise, don't post too little, or too much**

Timing isn't everything though—you need to know how much to post to Instagram too.

This is crucial because posting too much to Instagram will make your feed look inactive, while posting too much may raise concerns about your account being a spambot.

If you want to run with the big leagues, follow their lead alternate between posting once and twice per day.

❖ **Post photo albums that tell a story**

You probably already know that you can post multiple Instagram photos at once. But did you know you can use this feature to massively increase your engagement and the time people spend looking at your posts too?

Yup, it's possible and surprisingly simple to do too—make your multi-image posts tell a story. Here's how.

First, start with a punchy, eye-grabbing first image. This will draw your followers' attention and convince them to swipe through the rest of the images in your album. Then, make sure the rest of the images in your post are high-quality and flow together.

For example, you can make a post that shows the story of one of your products being developed. Or you can show someone how to make something new themselves—think arts and crafts, recipes, and other how-to's.

Then, once you've selected your images, add a cool caption that brings the photo album together. This can include a call-to-action or a "link in bio" that will encourage your followers to check out more of your content.

- ❖ **Keep an eye on what your competitors are posting**

No matter the social network, it's always important to keep tabs on what your competitors are posting to social media.

This will help you brainstorm new content ideas and find types of content that are working for others in your field.

In other words: let your competitors take the risk of posting new and experimental content for you, and take inspiration from what works for them.

Take a close look at what types of content performs best for your clients—in other words: look for posts with high numbers of likes and comments.

After you've found content that works for them, take your spin on it when reposting to your social feeds—never copy the same visual media or caption word-for-word.

❖ Add line breaks to your Instagram profile

Like breaks spice up Instagram profiles

One of the weird quirks of Instagram is that it doesn't let you use the return key when writing post captions or writing a bio in your profile. On iOS, for example, it simply doesn't give you the "return" key option on your keyboard.

This makes it seemingly impossible to write lists in your bio, so it's hard to format large chunks of content or separate things onto different lines.

Turns out, the return key reappears when you hit the 123 button on your iPhone's keyboard—and, amazingly enough, the return key works when pressed!

This means that you're free to add line breaks in your Instagram caption so that you can list out things like your business' location, new products, and even add phone numbers, and other ways to contact your business right in your bio.

Even cooler, this works in post captions too so that you can make multi-line captions and even divide up hashtags and the captions in your posts.

- ❖ **Use the tried-and-true like and follow strategy**

One of the easiest ways to grow your Instagram follower count is the tried-and-true like, and follow strategy. This is when you find an Instagram page similar to your own, follow it, and like a post or two.

Doing this will get your Instagram page in front of similar pages. This will encourage the admin of the page to follow you back and check out your content, in turn, building out your Instagram network and giving you useful connections within your industry.

Just one word of advice: make sure to do this manually and only follow accounts that are truly relevant to the types of content you post. Automation could get you banned from Instagram, and following accounts randomly won't provide any sort of benefit.

Oh, and one more thing: don't overdo this. If you follow hundreds of new accounts per day, you run the risk of looking like a bot. This can tank your brand image and ultimately ruin your Instagram presence.

- ❖ **Add Instagram follow buttons to your website, blog, and newsletters**

One of the easiest ways to build your Instagram following is by promoting your Instagram account on places where you already have a following—like your blog, website, and newsletter.

A way of doing this is by using a free tool like ShareThis to add Instagram follow buttons to your web properties. Grab the free button pack from their website, configure it with your social accounts, and you'll wrangle in new followers quickly.

- ❖ **Use Pexels to find free, high-quality Instagram content**

Don't have the time to create original photo and video content? Don't write off Instagram yet. Instead, use a high-quality free image repository like Pexels to find premade content that you can post without charge or attribution.

Pexels curates content from all of the web's biggest royalty free image sites, giving you tens-of-thousands of images and video clips that you can repost to your own Instagram feed without charge.

You can post these to your Instagram account when you're out of ideas, or when your content library has run dry.

Just make sure that you mix this content up with actual in-house content so that you get the upside of posting original content while still posting consistently.

❖ Play with Instagram story stickers

Likewise, make sure you're using all of the available stories features when you create Instagram stories on your account. Namely, add interactive Instagram stickers like quizzes, Q&A, and polls to your stories.

These stickers give your audience a super easy way to interact with your brand. For example, someone can vote on a poll in seconds when tapping through your Instagram story as they don't have to type or take a photo of anything.

Plus, these stickers also make your audience feel like you care about their opinion. So, use them often, and you'll see a nice boost in engagement and the public's perception of your brand.

- ❖ **Experiment with a private account (with caution)**

Recently, some brands have had success gaining (and retaining) followers by using a private Instagram account. The thinking here is that people will be enticed by your private profile and that they'll think twice before unfollowing.

However, the harsh reality here is that most brands and influencers shouldn't have a private Instagram account.

Nowadays, brands and influencers need a public-facing Instagram account to build a brand. And unless you're getting a ton of private message shares, there's a good chance your growth will stagnate compared when using a private account.

- ❖ **Start posting videos regularly**

Videos are huge on Instagram. From 2017 to 2018, Instagram video views more than quadrupled. This signals that Instagram users are not only posting more video content, but crave more of it too.

Use this to your advantage and post more videos to your Instagram feed. These can be as simple as a quick office tour to a full-blown edited video interview with a well-known influencer in your industry.

Whatever you do though, make sure that you're posting short and punchy content that can be digested easily. There's a strict one-minute video length limit on Instagram, and we've found that the shorter the video, the more views and engagements it gets.

- ❖ **Schedule your Instagram posts in advance**

If you're new to Instagram marketing, there's a good chance that you're managing Instagram differently than the rest of the social networks you post to. So while you may have a Twitter and Facebook scheduling tool, and you're likely posting Instagram direct from your phone.

This presents a myriad of issues. If you're on vacation, for example, you can't set your Instagram app to auto-post for you. Instead, you'll have to manually log on and post your new Instagram post, interrupting your vacation in the process.

But what if we told you there was an easier way? A way so easy that it doesn't even require a smartphone to post?

❖ **Track your Instagram growth**

Track your growth with an Instagram analytics tool.

So, you've successfully built an Instagram marketing strategy and put all of these Instagram hacks into play, but how do you know that they're working?

Simple: you need an awesome Instagram analytics tool.

You can use these tools to track your follower growth, total engagements, and other key metrics. Then, you can examine this data, and see if your Instagram strategy is working, or if you need to make some edits and re-imagine your strategy.

www.ingramcontent.com/pod-product-compliance
Lightning Source LLC
Chambersburg PA
CBHW060832220526
45466CB00003B/1070